FRAGMENTS OF CLARITY

Chloie Green

Roots & Echoes

ROOTS & ECHOES

To Ruth.

Thank you for always being so friendly and welcoming. Even though we dont talk often, your smile and kindness always make Bridewell feel that little bit brighter and easier to walk into.

Love
Chloie x.

ISBN-13: 9798246130070

Cover design by: Art Painter
Library of Congress Control Number: 2018675309
Printed in the United States of America

I created this image while I spent time in a mental home.
It is the inspiration that lead me to writing this book.

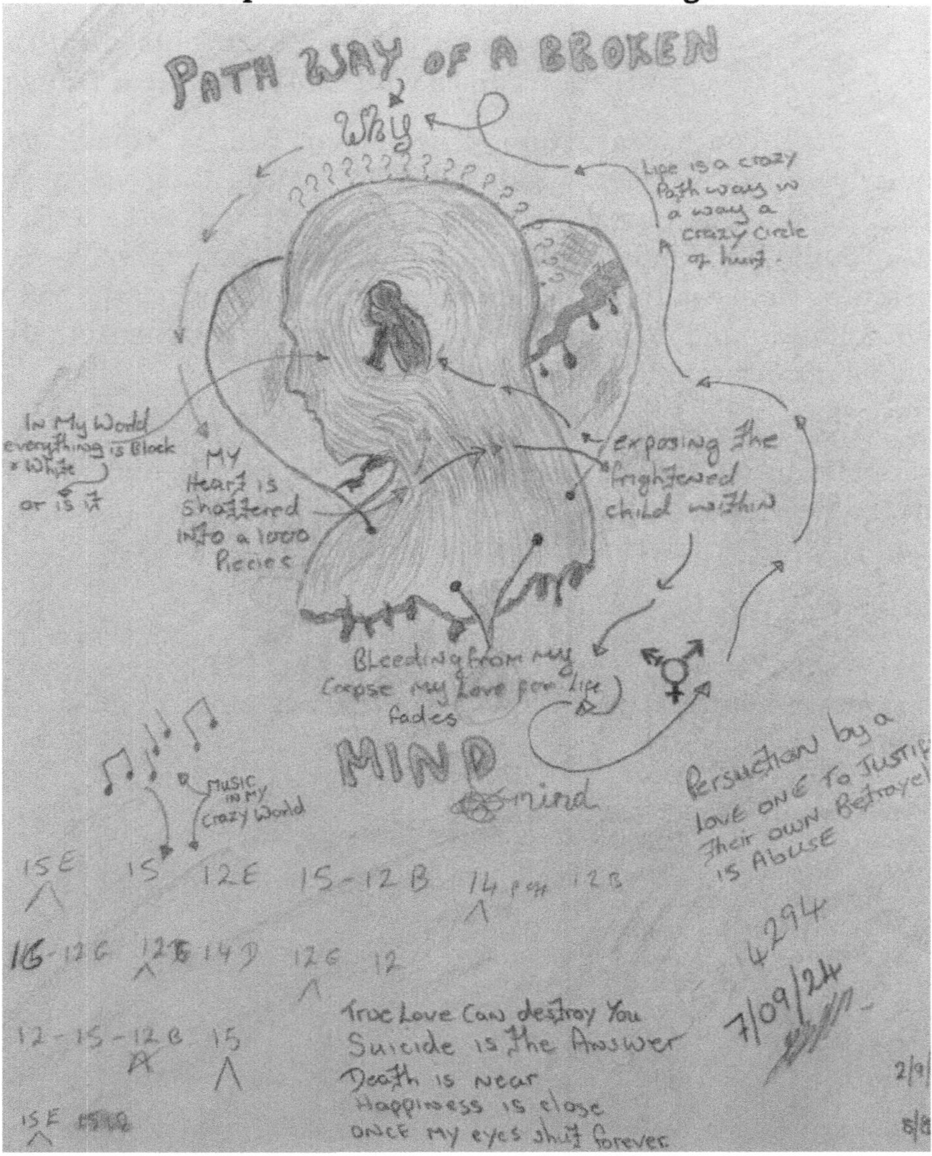

Acknowledgements

For Paul,

In Loving memory of an amazing bloke with a gentle heart and a wild love for the little things

Paul, you had a nature all your own, kind, curious, and quietly full of wonder. I will never forget the time we were cleaning out that rancid old water butt. Your hands were wrists deep in the slime and the stink, and while I was gagging, you were grinning from ear to ear, and absolutely buzzing about all the bugs wriggling around in there. That was you. Finding joy where others would not even think of looking.

You read my stories, these stories when they were just scribbles in my journal. You told me they mattered, and would help others. You told me to share them. “You should get these out there, get them published," you said.

Well here they are, I did it.

This book is for you, for your laughter, your encouragement, and your way of seeing the overlooked. I miss you mate. I always will.

Chloie.

Prologue

There was a time when everything I knew, everything I loved, fell apart.

I lost a job I was passionate about. I lost the person I thought I would spend my life with. And somewhere in the middle of that collapse, I lost myself. I was sectioned twice under the Mental Health Act. I became homeless. I became suicidal. And in the darkest moments, I truly believed I would not make it out.

What hurt the most was not just the pain, It was the silence that surrounded it. The feeling of being invisible in a system meant to help. The cold clinical care that left me feeling like a number rather than a person. I realised something that still breaks my heart: sometimes, the mental health system does not save you.

But someone did.

A peer support worker, someone, who had walked their own path through pain, sat with me and spoke to me like a human being. No clipboard, no rush, no judgement. And for the first time in a long time, I did not feel alone.

That moment changed everything.

I started writing a journal, not with the intention of creating anything, just to survive. The entries slowly became something else. They became short stories. Pieces of my truth told through other voices in my own mind. Reflections of real pain, real heartbreak, real confusion, and eventually, real healing.

A friend of mine, before he took his own life, read those stories and said:

"You should get these out there."

This book is for him. And for anyone who has ever stood on the edge wondering if it is worth holding on.

Every story in this book carries something real: the weight of pain, the slow burn of healing, and most importantly, the quiet, stubborn presence of hope.

If you are reading this, come as you are, These stories may hurt sometimes. But they are honest. And if nothing else, let them remind you that you are not alone.

The Effort 1

The alarm goes off, I do not know what time it is, I do not want to know. I just know it is morning because the light through the window is too harsh. I stare at the ceiling, I tell myself just sit up, that it is one motion, but my body does not listen. It feels like I am pinned under something heavy, invisible, constant.

The thought of standing up, brushing my teeth, pretending to care, is unbearable. And yet somehow I manage it. Even worse though is the thought of another day wasted, another unanswered text, another excuse, another friend quietly giving up on me, why do i look at my phone, just waiting for a reply, thinking the worse.

My phone buzzes and I look at the message. *Are you still coming today?* I stare at the screen until it goes dark again. They will judge me if I show up like this: Eyes puffy, silent, answers too loud, answers too flat, answers too abrupt. But they will judge me if I do not show up too.

No one says it, but I feel it, you are not trying hard enough. If only they knew how hard it is just to exist, to breathe, to vanish completely. I roll onto my side, that is something right? Maybe tomorrow I will get up...

MAYBE.

Later I saw the photos. Three of them at the cafe we all used to go to together including me. Laughing, sunlight pouring through the window golden and soft. someone iced coffee sweating on the table, a bite taken out of a croissant.

They tagged me.

I do not not like the post, I want to, I really want to be there. God I miss them, not just them, the me I was when I could be with them.

I imagine how it would have gone if I had forced myself out of the door. I would have sat quietly, smiling in the right places, drinking something I barely tasted. I would have pretended everything was fine. Maybe they would have believed me, maybe not, either way, I would have gone home exhausted, ashamed, and hollow.

But this...

This is worse.

I scroll through the comments, inside jokes. *We missed you!* One of them writes. Did they? Did they really?

Because here is the truth I never say;

I am not avoiding them because I do not care. I am avoiding them because I care too much, and I can not bear to show up as this version of myself. The dull one, the quiet one, the one who used to be fun, used to be alive.

I stare at the reflection in the black screen. I want to scream, I want to cry, but mostly, I just want to be ok.

I close my eyes and imagine sitting with them again, not performing, not pretending, just there, just being me.

But I do not know who that is any more.

The Effort 2

The worst part is not the loneliness. It is the voice in my head that tells me I deserve this. That voice is always there, whispering like static behind everything.

You are a burden.
You are too much.
You are not enough.

It never makes up its mind, just loops endlessly, picking at me like fingers at a scab.

I try to remember when this started, there was not a single moment, some dramatic fall (not at first, that came later). It was quieter than that. Like sinking into quicksand one slow inch at a time, until I could not tell when I stopped trying to get out.

I still laugh sometimesI still smile that confuses people. But smiling is not healing, it is hiding, it is survival. Because if I let the sadness show. Really show. I am afraid it will never stop.

I think about the people I really love, my children, Her, Family, Friends. I think about how much they mean to me, laugh without me now, how they carry on. I am not mad at them for it. I might have done the same.

I think about how if i disappeared, they would be sad for a while. Then life would go on, quietly, reshaping itself around my absence, just a memory, like water filling in after a stone is removed. I hate myself for thinking that, but I think about it all the time anyway.

And still there is a part of me that wants out. Not out of life, not really.

Out of this feeling, out of this body that drags like an anchor. Out of the haze that makes joy feel like something that belongs to other people.

I want to get better.
I just do not know how.

The Effort 3

It was quiet in the hospital, even with the machines humming. They put me in a room with soft walls and nothing sharp. I remember the cold vinyl mattress, the weight of nothing to do but think. I do not know what I said or what I did to get sectioned, maybe I did not have too much, maybe my eyes said it all.

The hours blurred, nurses came and went, soft voiced and careful. I counted ceiling tiles, I imagined what the world was doing without me. I wondered if they even noticed I had gone.

Then a knock on the door, not from a nurse, the door creaked open and there they were, my friends, not smiling, not saying anything clever. Just standing there holding plastic coffee cups and an awkward hope.

They sat beside me like they did not know what to say, but also like they did not need to say anything. One of them reached out, their hand brushing mine like it might break if they pressed too hard. "I am glad you are still here," one whispered.

I wanted to cry but the tears would not come, so I nodded that was all I had in me. We sat like that for a while, no small talk, no pressure to explain, just presence.

That moment sits in me like a small, flickering light. Even now, when the fog fades in and I fade back into the black i remember it. They showed up, they came for me. Even when I could not come for myself.

And yet even now, I struggle to reach out. Not because I do not trust them, but because shame wraps around me like ivy growing up a tree. Whispering they have done enough. Don't make them carry more.

Still I sometimes wonder what would happen if I just said, "I am not okay, can we talk?" not to explain, not to fix, just not to be alone.

The Effort 4

It has been days since I answered anyone. My phone was a black mirror on the bedside cabinet, untouched except to check the time and then regret knowing it. Then a vibration, not a notification, a message from Julie.

Hey, no pressure, just thinking of you today.
I am around if you ever want to talk, or sit, or just be quiet together.

I stare at it for so long the screen dims. No emojis, no guilt, no where have you been? Just an open door.

And somehow that helped, more than any apology or plea could have. It is the silence between the words that matters. The quiet kind of love that does not demand only waits. I want to reply, but the words do not come easily. I type and retype and erase five drafts. And finally, I sent it.

Thank you, I am not Okay, but I want to be.

It is not elegant, it is not even a conversation. But it is honest, it is real, it is the best I can do for now. And when the message shows as read, I wait not for an answer, but for the simple truth that I reached out. That for once the darkness did not win.

Moments later.

That is enough, I am here.
Six words: simple and solid.

I press the phone to my chest like it might anchor me to the world. And for the first time in what feels like forever. I do not feel like I am falling, just resting, held, seen.

Tomorrow the effort will still be there, the darkness, the disappearance will not disappear overnight. But maybe, just maybe I will not have to carry it alone.

The Effort 5

The next day I got out of bed, not in a triumphant movie, montage kind of way. More like I sit up, I swing my legs over the edge. I stare at the floor for ten minutes then I stand. Wobbly at first, like I am relearning how to be human. I brush my teeth, have a wash, and it feels like victory and defeat at the same time. But I am up.

Later that day I met Julie at the park, not a crowded place, just a quiet patch of grass near a bench we used to sit on. When I arrived, I thought about turning around. I imagine a hundred she might say, a thousand ways I might disappoint. But Julie just smiles, not wide, not exaggerated, just soft, real.

"Hey she says." And it is enough.

We sit, we talk a little and sit more. She does not ask me to explain. She will not fix anything. She just stays, and when I say, "It has been really bad." She just nods, "I know she replies, I am just glad you are still here."

We do not stay long, I get tired easily these days. But before I leave, Julie pulls something from her bag, a small notebook. Blank pages, the kind that waits for new words.

"For when you are ready." She says, "No rush." I hold it in both hands like it might break or save me. Later back in bed I flip through it, nothing inside but space, possibility. But now if you are reading this book, you know what the pages became filled with over time.

I know there will be more hard days, days when the bed feels like quicksand again. When silence stretches too long and the darkness comes back heavier than ever. But now, there is a thread tying me to the world, a message, a bench, a notebook with blank pages. And most importantly a friend who does need me to be fixed, just here.

Healing is not loud, it is not fast, it has its ups and downs. Sometimes it looks like getting out of bed, sometimes it is just staying trying to belong.

And for now staying is enough.

Survival

I sit in the shower longer than I should, let the water run until the mirror fogs over and the heat fades. My skin turns red, but it is the only thing that reminds me I am still here, still inside this body I still fight with every day.

After I towel myself off I catch a glimpse of myself in the mirror. And I see not the face I show the world, not the version that says, "I am fine." But the raw version, the one I only see when the mask slips. My eyes drop to my wrists. The scars are there, maybe faint now, but they are a reminder of dark days, and destruction of myself. There are some faint, some thinner than thread, some deeper, stitch marks some faded but they are there and they scream.

I remember the night they happened, not the details, just the feeling. That heavy silence, the belief that nothing would ever change, that I was too broken to be fixed. That the world would keep spinning whether I stayed or not.

But I am still here.

That thought both hurts and heals at the same time.

I used to hide my arms, even in summer. Long sleeves, excuses, shadows. I was terrified of what people would think, of being labelled, pitied, avoided. But now I look at these marks and see something else.

Survival.

They are not a sign of weakness, they are proof I fought my way through a storm that nearly swallowed me whole. They are reminders that pain does not always win. That I did not give up, even when I wanted to.

Underneath my skin, beneath the weight of the sadness and the smile I wear like armour. I am just like anyone else, I bleed, I break, I feel too much, I long to be understood, long to be listened to, long to be held, without having to explain why I am not okay.

I am not the happy, normal person people think they see.

But maybe I do not have to be. Maybe healing is not about becoming someone else, maybe it is about learning to live as myself, scars and all.

Somedays the darkness still whispers, but now I have louder voices. The friend who texted, the kid inside me who sees a monkey, the dog that curls up against me, like I am made of something good. And maybe, just maybe I am starting to believe that too.

So nowadays I step outside, no sleeves, no apologies, just me. Why? Because I survived, because I am still learning and because today that is enough.

It is a Monday afternoon when I see her, sitting alone in the church yard, sleeves pulled past her hands, staring at the ground like it might swallow her whole. Something about her posture, her stillness, it is familiar too familiar.

I hesitate, I am not a saviour, I am not fixed. Hell I barely made it through last week without falling apart. But something inside me knows that silence, that ache, that need for someone just to see you, and not look away. Someone to hear you and just listen, someone just to say it is ok not to be ok.

So I sat down beside her, a few feet of space between us, quiet, no big gesture, no deep words, just sitting there in silence to start off with.

After a few minutes I say, “It gets loud sometimes doesn't it.” She does not look up, but I see her shoulders shift, like taking a breath she had been holding just to let go. “Yeah,” she whispers.

We do not talk about the details, I do not ask her what is wrong, she does not explain. But that is not the point, the point is we are not alone anymore.

I roll up my sleeves without thinking, the scars catch the sunlight, I do not say anything I do not have too. She notices, her eyes flicker and for the first time her eyes meet mine, she is looking at me like she can see my soul.

There is no pity there, no shock, just quiet recognition, a mutual understanding, between two people who made it, to the other side of something dark. I do not know what she will do next,

I do not know if i helped. But I know I showed up. I gave her what I did not have back then. A presence, a breath, a handrail, a hope.

That night I sat on my bed, the same spot where I once thought it might all end. And I cry again, but it is different now. Lighter there is grief, yes but also something warm beside it- HOPE.

I am not fixed, not cured. But I am alive, and I have learned that maybe nothing else matters, not perfection, not pretending not performing, except that I stayed, and I will keep staying. One breath, one scar, one step at a time, one day at a time and that is what survivors do.

Letting The Light In

A week passes, the girl from the bench, her name is irrelevant. We talk now, not everyday, not about everything, but enough. Enough to know we have both stood on the edge, enough to know we do not have to anymore.

Today I am the one sitting on the edge, this time on my own bed, phone in my hand screen lit up with her name. My thumb hovers over the call button. It should not be this hard, but reaching out always feels like an apology, like I am a burden. Like I am asking for more than I deserve. But then I remember something she said a few days ago, "You showed up when I did not even know I needed someone, do not ever think that is small."

So I pressed the button, "Hello," I said, voice tight in my throat." She replies with, "Hello," and, "You ok." I pause and let the question settle. "No, I say. Not really." There is silence on the other end of the phone, but it is not uncomfortable, it is just space. Space for me to keep going, if I wanted to, and I do.

"I feel like I am slipping again, and I do not want to lie about it anymore."

"Okay," she replies softly. "Do you want to meet up?"

"Yes please." I whispered.

We meet up and hardly speak, barely touched, we do not do anything profound, just sit, side by side two people with cracks in their armour and enough courage to admit it.

I roll up my sleeves without shame now. My scars have become a kind of language now. They speak of pain yes, but also of the fight, the survival, the choice to stay. "I used to think I was broken," I tell her and she looks at me. "You are not, you are healing." I nod but the words feel foreign, strange. I am still learning how to wear them.

Later when we part I go back to the sanctuary of my home, and I stare at the quiet of my room, I realize something.

It does not feel empty anymore. Maybe healing is not a straight line, maybe it is more like this, messy conversation, showing up when it is hard, letting people see the parts we think disqualify us from love. Maybe letting the light in is not about throwing the door wide open. Maybe it starts with the door slightly open. And maybe, for the first time I am okay with that.

Roots Of Hope

I never expected to survive that night.

After taking the tablets, I felt an overwhelming weight pressing down on my chest. The world seemed to close in, and I believed I had reached the end. My thoughts were not loud or dramatic, they were quiet, almost numb, like static. Like after the power cuts out.

Standing on that bridge, staring into the dark below, I was not contemplating life or death. I just wanted the pain to stop. I wanted to disappear.

And then I stepped off.

But fate had other plans. A police officer grabbed me, pulling me back from the edge. I do not remember the force of his grip, that moment I resented him for saving me. I wanted to be left alone to be left alone in my despair.

The next thing I knew, I woke up in a hospital bed. IVs in my arm, Heart monitors connected to me, bright lights above, and a sense of confusion clouding my mind. I felt ashamed, angry and lost, but amidst the turmoil, a small voice whispered, "What do we know?"

Recovery did not come in a rush, it was slow, painful and often felt like two steps forward and one step back. Some days I did not speak, most nights I did not sleep. But then the mental health team introduced me to Bridewell, the mental health garden for recovery.

At first I did not care, it was just another program, another way to pass the time. I went, I stood there detached, anxious, barely touching the tools. The others seemed so engaged, so alive, I felt like an outsider in my own skin.

But something shifted over time. Maybe it was the soil under my nails, the way the sun warmed my face or the quiet conversations with others who understood. There was the man who had been sober for a few years now, who was doing so well, but still had bad days. There was a woman who had tried to end her life twice, and now she planted sun flowers every spring. Just to bring sunshine into her life, and to remind herself how far she had come.

Their stories did not fix me, but they made me feel less alone, and gave me hope for the future.

In the garden, things grow slowly, you water, you wait, you prune, you celebrate. I realised I was not broken, I was buried. And maybe, just maybe I could grow too.

One day I looked around and saw others tending their little patches, some silent, some laughing, some crying. But all were healing, I looked down at the seedlings I had planted weeks ago, now rising through the dirt. And I felt something I had not felt in a long time- HOPE.

Not the loud flashy kind, but the quiet steady kind. The kind that whispers, you are still here, and that matters.

Today I still have dark moments, I still struggle, but I also have roots. I have people around me who understand, I have a garden that I love going to. And most importantly I have friends, and hope. Not because everything is perfect, but because I am growing day by day alongside others. Others who remind us that we are not alone in our pain, or in our healing.

I am still here, we are still here and you are still here, and sometimes that is enough.

The Darkness

The first time it came, I was way too young to name it. It was not sadness, not at first it was more like a silence that settled in places, sound used to live. But now it is just darkness, like someone has dimmed the lights behind my eyes. I remember lying in bed at night too wired to sleep, but too numb to move. Feeling a pressure in my chest, like something pressing me down.

People around me did not notice, I still smiled, still answered questions. But inside me something had shifted, I started to feel like I was not really there, people could not hear me. I felt like I was just watching myself go through the motions, day after day, and slowly not feeling like I existed.

I did not know it then, but that was the beginning. The darkness did not announce itself, it slipped in quietly. Gently at first, the way dusk bleeds into the night. Before I knew it, I was drowning in it.

There were moments when fear would jolt me back, like waking from a dream you cannot quite remember. But I am sure it was trying to tell me something important. One night gripped by panic in a room that felt too loud and too silent at the same time, I curled into myself and felt something crack. Not physically, something deeper.

That was the first time I reached out for escape.

The Darkness 2

That first cut was quiet, a single line shallow and fast, the blood did not matter. What mattered was the pain, now had a place outside of me. Something visible, something real. It was like proving to myself that I was not making it all up. That,what I was feeling inside, deserved to exist.

It was not an act of giving up, it was a way to keep going.

That is the part people do not understand. Sometimes the darkest things we do are not about wanting to die, but desperately needing to stay alive. The wound healed but something opened in its place, an awareness. A recognition that I was fighting something bigger than sadness. That I was living with a shadow that did not want to kill me, but did not want me to fully live either.

The darkness would return again and again, and each time it came with another cut. But it also brought something else, a deeper understanding, a quieter kind of strength. I began to notice things others did not, the way the morning light bent through a cracked window, the way music filled a room like breath. The softness in someone's voice when they say your name and mean it.

My pain did not vanish, but I learned to walk beside it.

Fear stopped being a monster in the corner. It became a companion, it reminded me, I was still alive, that I was choosing to stay. Even when it hurts, especially when it hurts.

I do not pretend to be healed, that is not the point. The point is I am still here.

I learned how to sit in the dark, without letting it swallow me. I learned that survival is not clean or pretty, it is raw, it is messy, but it is real and it is sacred.

Some nights, the shadows still visit, but I do not fight it anymore. I light a candle, I breathe deep, I listen. Because now I know.

The darkness did not break me, it made me see.

And I am still here.

The Mirror Named True

There was once a small child who lived in a quiet little village, where everything had a place, and everyone believed they knew who you were before you even spoke. To them the little girl was just a boy.

They gave her trucks and blue clothes and called her young man, smiling like they gave her something wonderful. But the child did not smile back. Not really because deep down, quietly, clearly, and without question she knew she was a girl.

I tried to tell them once, "I am not a boy," I said softly.

They laughed, or went quiet, or said things like, "Do not be silly," so I stopped saying it out loud. But I never stopped knowing.

There was only one place I felt safe to be myself, the attic of my Nan's house, where an old mirror stood tall and waiting. Its frame was carved with roses and vines, and though a crack ran through one corner, it had never lied.

When I stood before it, the world outside it disappeared. And the girl inside the mirror looked back. She had soft eyes and gentle hands. Her hair fell in curls, sometimes waves or braids, it just depended on the day. Sometimes she wore dresses made of starlight, she danced, sometimes she just stood still and smiled.

"Hello," the reflection would whisper. "I see you," and that meant everything to me.

But the world outside of the attic was loud. It kept calling me something I was not, they still do. Kept pushing me into being something I was not. Over time I visited the mirror less and less. Not because I stopped believing, but believing had started to hurt.

I eventually grew up.

People still used the wrong name, the wrong words, they still thought they knew me, and I tried so hard to be what they wanted, just to survive. But it came with a cost, a deep sadness I did not always understand, anger, silence, emptiness, the start of darkness that consumed my thoughts, still consumes my thoughts to this day.

There were years I spent learning how to live with the sadness, years spent in therapy rooms, thoughts in journals, time spent in silence, there were moments of joy too, bright and defiant, but the hurt never left, not really. But I still had memories of the mirror. The memory of the mirror still reminds me of my thoughts still, not the wood or the glass, but the truth it had shown me.

One day years later I stood in front of a mirror again, this time in my own home. My reflection was not perfect, I still carried scars, still had the darkness inside me. But I wore my own name now, my own clothes, my own truths.

I looked at myself in the mirror, looked myself in the eye and said out loud, "I am still here," I have survived up to now. So maybe, just maybe I can survive the darkness now.

And myself in the mirror, the girl I have always been, smiled back at me with hope.

Remember or not

I wake up to white light and the bleeping of machines. My arms are full of bruises and tape. Again I do not know where I am, but the smell and the noises tell me it is a hospital.

I ask the nurse what happened, but she looks at me like I should know.

"You overdosed again," she says gently. AGAIN.

There are whole weeks missing from my memory, holes, blackouts. People tell me I did things, phoned them, shouted, walked barefoot up the motorway in the rain. The police said I looked calm when they found me. Like I was on my way somewhere, like I knew where I was going. But I did not, I do not know.

Sometimes people come up to me and talk like we have had conversations before, like we have laughed or argued or cried together. But I have no idea who they are, no idea what they are talking about. I smile and nod, trying not to show the panic clawing at my insides.

My ex wife said I was like Jekyll and Hyde. One moment I am quiet, trying to hold it together, the next I am a stranger, cold or chaotic, absent.

And when I come back from wherever my head goes, I find the wreckage of what I have done, the people I have hurt, the bridges burned. And I do not even remember lighting the match.

The scariest part is not what I have done, it is the not knowing, the wondering, the fear that maybe one day, I will not wake up, I will not come back at all, I will not exist anymore.

Fifteen Minutes

3:02pm

The silence in my house is not peaceful, it is heavy, thick like fog that will not lift. Some days I feel like the walls are closing in, not of menace, but out of sheer emptiness. The stillness amplifies every thought in my head until they are too loud, too sharp, too overwhelming.

I go and sit on my sofa, not doing anything, just staring, I have not spoken a word all day, there is no one to speak to, and even if there was, I am not sure I would not know what to say anyway. Talking feels like another language now an unspoken world.

I glance at my clock on the shelf.

3:17pm

It feels like I have been sitting here forever, hours at least, but the clock says otherwise.

I tell myself I will go out tomorrow, just outside, just for a minute. But when the time comes, the fear grips me tight. The idea of the world out there, people, noise, sunlight, judgement, feels too big. I pull the curtains instead, I scroll through my phone, though I barely read anything, plans get ignored, messages stay unread, I sink deeper.

One day I picked up a pen and sketched a door on the back of an old envelope, just a simple rectangle. Then I drew my hand on the handle, my foot stepping out. I imagined it like a story, like it was happening to someone else, someone braver than me.

I kept that drawing by the door for days, maybe weeks. I looked at it every time I passed, and each time, I tried to picture it for real. Opening the door, taking that first step.

Then one afternoon I did.

It was slow, I stood in the hallway for what felt like an hour. My hand shook as I reached for the handle. When I opened the door, even the light in the hallway felt loud, but I stepped out.

I heard my neighbours door open and I froze. She looked at me and smiled softly, like she knew not to push. "Are you alright," she asked gently.

I nodded, even though my heart was hammering. She did not press, she just nodded back and walked on, like it was no big deal. But to me it was everything. Her voice reminded me I was not invisible, that the world was still there, and maybe it had not forgotten me.

Those first steps were terrifying, my legs felt weak, my breath too fast. But I kept walking, just to the end of the block and back. It was not much, but it was more than nothing. More than I had done in weeks, maybe months.

Now I go out a little more, to the shop, to grab a coffee, even to just sit on a bench and breathe in the outside air. Each time it takes something from me, a little push a quiet argument with the fear, but I do it. It is still scary... Sometimes my chest tightens before I even reach the door, sometimes I turn back. But I have learned that even the smallest steps count.

The drawing of the door is still there, taped to my wall a reminder that I made it out once, and that I can do it again.

Even if it takes everything I have got.

Stillness Between Stars (poem)

There is a silence that hums
In the spaces where your name
Use to echo
Not absence
But a presence made of memories breath

Time does not move the way it once did
Now it drips
Slow and silver
Through the branches of
Something i cannot name

I reach out, not to grasp
But to feel the wind your shadow
Leaves behind
And in that hush
I learn how to carry love without holding it

Maybe we were not meant to end
Only to pause
In the stillness between stars
Waiting for a sky wide enough
To meet again

The Room Without A Light Switch

I lie in bed, eyes closed, still as stone, but inside, it is loud, it always is.

My brain does not shut off, it never has. Thoughts crawl in like vines, wrapping around everything, tugging me backwards, sideways into memories, I do not wish to relive and futures I am terrified to face.

The voices come next, not strangers, not echoes of other people. They are all me.

One is a little girl, crying softly, "Why did they leave? Did I do something wrong?"

Another is a teenager, angry and lost, spitting out blame, "This is your fault, you let this happen, you let us become this."

Then comes the twenty something version of me, exhausted and fake smiling through a life that feels like borrowed cloth. "If you do not hold it all together, no one will, do not fall apart. Not again."

And sometimes there is an older voice, one I have not even grown into yet, Bitter, resigned.

"It never got better, you just got used to the noise."

They argue, they pile on, they replay moments like movies with no pause button. Things I said wrong, things I did not say, things I never got over.

I try breathing, counting, grounding, listening to calming music tricks I learned from books, and therapists and midnight google searches, but the voices do not care about coping strategies. They have been with me longer than sleep ever has.

I wake up tired in ways I cannot explain, like I thought battles in dreams I cannot remember, like I had to carry every version of myself on my back just to make it through to morning.

People say, "It is just overthinking, you need to relax."

But they do not live in this mind, a house with a thousand rooms and no doors.

They do not hear the 7 year old me sobbing in one corner, all she wants to do is play, while the twenty year old me spirals out of control. They do not know what it is like when your own thoughts sound like ghosts. Every night I hope maybe tonight will be the one, maybe the voices will rest.

Maybe I will get a moment of peace.
But I am still waiting,
Still wide awake in the room,
Without a light switch.

CHLOIE GREEN

The Bench In The Rain

I come here when the noise gets too loud.

Not the outside world, though also that has its own endless chaos, but the storm inside of me, the thoughts that ricochet, the weight that does not lift, the ache that does not announce itself but never quite goes away.

This bench tucked away beneath the old oak tree in the corner of the cemetery. Has become my quiet place, my little harbour. I have sat here in the sun, wind and very often like today even in the rain.

It is not pouring, just that slow steady never ending drizzle that makes everything smell like earth and memory. I like it, it keeps most people away, except today, someone else is here,

They are sitting on the far end of the bench, shoulders hunched, hoodie pulled up, hands clenched around a paper cup that might have been coffee. They are not looking at me, not really looking at anything. Just staring out over the empty grass, over the graves like they are waiting for something that probably won't come.

I glance over, then away. I do not want to intrude, but something about the way they are sitting, rigid, brittle, like one more thought could break them open, pulls at something inside of me.

I know that posture.

I wore it for a long time.

My heart tugs forward, but my feet stay planted. I do not know what to say, what if i say the wrong thing? What if I make it worse? What if they are drowning and all I have is a paper cup.

I sigh and shift slightly, enough to be visible in their peripheral vision. I do not move closer, I just let myself exist beside them. Silent, long, heavy, but not empty.

Finally I speak out loud, not soft, just enough, “Are you okay?”

Their head moves a fraction, then a shrug, “I guess.” That is the thing about that answer, “I guess,” is a way of saying no without having to say it. It is how we say, “I am not fine, but I do not want to talk about it,” and, “Please notice but do not push.”

So I nod like I understand, because I do.

A few minutes pass, the rain patters on the leaves above us and we sit in it. Not together but not alone either.

“I used to come here when things were really bad,” I said eventually. “Still do sometimes, this bench kind of held me, when I thought nothing else could.”

She did not respond but she shifted just slightly, a signal of a subtle opening.

“I did not know how to ask for help back then, I thought I would be a burden. Or that no one would understand.” I pause, unsure if I should keep going, then, “Truth is most people did not understand.” That gets a tiny laugh, bitter but real, I smile faintly. “Yea, it sucked.”

A little more time of silence. “I am tired.” She said just that. I nod again. “Yea, I know, that tired. The kind that sleep does not fix.” She glanced at me for the first time, just for a second, eyes dark, rimmed with that raw kind of hurt that no one talks about.

“I do not want advice,” she muttered.

“I was not going to give any,” I said, “I just don't want you to feel invisible.”

That made her go still, like maybe that hit closer than they expected. Another long pause then softly, “Thank you,”

It is barely above a whisper, like a secret, or a prayer. I do not say anything back, just sit, just stay. Sometimes presence is all we can offer, sometimes it is enough.

Eventually she stood up, pulled her hoodie tighter, “I will see you around,” she said and for the first time there was something in her voice that was not there before. A thread of possibility.

I watched her walk away through the misty rain. I do not know where she is going, I do not know what comes next for her. But I know this, even if I could not fix anything today, she was not alone.

And maybe, just maybe, that made a difference.

The Bench In The Rain

Chapter 2- The Girl With The Scars.

The rain had stopped, it felt like it had lasted for days.

It left behind that smell I always liked, the kind that makes everything feel clean, even if nothing's really changed.

I came back to the bench, the one under the old oak, not expecting anything, just quiet, maybe to breathe, take a break, reflect. But she was already there. She looked young, maybe 20 to 25, wearing a threadbare sweatshirt and black leggings with holes in the knees. Her hair was knotted like she had given up brushing it days ago. Her arms were crossed, sleeves pulled tight.

But I saw them.

The faint lines that peeked from under the fabric, crisscrossed like faded roads on pale skin. She noticed me noticing, her eyes flicked to mine, defiant like a challenge. I did not flinch, did not look away either, I just sat at the other end of the bench.

The silence between us stretched, but it was not uncomfortable, more like cautious, two people walking a tightrope between being strangers and something else.

“I am not a charity case,” she muttered eventually. “I did not think you were,” I replied. She side eyed me. “Are you going to tell me it gets better or something?”

“No,” I said, “Not unless you want me to lie.”

That made her blink, then for a moment she almost smiled, Almost. “So what then?” She asked, “Are you here to watch me fall apart?”

“No,” I said gently, “I am just here.”

She stared out across the empty graveyard, the wind picked up and she shivered a little, but she did not adjust her hoodie. After a long pause, she spoke again, voice quieter this time, “It is not for attention.”

“I know,” I replied.

"I mean, I do not even want people to see them," she pulled her sleeve down reflexively. "I just don't know what else to do with it all, the noise."

I nodded, "Yea, the kind that builds up until it needs somewhere to go." She glanced at me again, "You ever?" she did not finish the question, she did not have to. I nodded again, "Yea, I have had my own ways of bleeding some can be seen. Others, no one could see."

That hit something in her, her eyes shimmered. Not crying, but close, not breaking, but bending.

"I am tired," she whispered. "All the time, and angry and then I feel guilty for being angry, and then I am just numb."

"I hear you."

She stared at me for a long time, like she did not know whether to trust me, or maybe whether to trust anyone who could actually understand. And maybe she did not trust, but she did not leave either.

"You are not trying to fix me?" she asked.

"Nope."

"Why?"

"Because I am not here to fix you," I said. "Just to sit with you however long you need."

Silence once again, then very softly, "Thank you."

It was barely a breath. I did not say anything back, just stayed there, still, quiet, present.

After a while she stood, she did not look at me when she left, but she did not cover her scars either.

And somehow, that felt like something.

End Note:

We do not always need answers. Most of us already know there is no quick fix, no magic, words that make the weight disappear.

Sometimes, what we need more than anything is to be seen, heard, to have someone sit beside us in silence. To know we are not alone in the dark, even if no one has a map out of it.

This story is not about solving anything, it is a true story, it is about showing up.

Because presence without judgement, without pressure is powerful.

Sometimes just having someone say, "I am here, I see you." is enough to keep us going one more day. So if you are struggling, you do not have to explain yourself, you do not have to be strong, you just have to keep breathing one minute at a time.

And if you are the one sitting beside someone hurting, you do not need the perfect words, you do not need a solution, just be there quiet, steady, human.

Sometimes that is the most healing thing we can offer.

AUTHOR NOTES

I have been there too, I am still there.

I have sat in silence, unsure how to ask for help. I have felt the weight of sadness I could not explain, and the guilt that followed it. I have wanted to help others more than I knew how, because I understand what the pain feels like, and how lonely it can be.

If you are going through it right now, I want you to know, you are not weak, you are not broken. You are surviving something incredibly heavy, and that takes real strength, even when it does not feel like it.

And if you are the one trying to support someone else, but feel helpless. Please remember that just being there matters more than you know, you do not have to fix anything, just showing up quietly, patiently, without judgement is already an act of love.

Thank you for reading this, I hope in some small way it helped you feel seen, or reminded you to keep going.

You are not alone.

Chloie.

Above The Thermals

I am a buzzard.

I do not remember when I stopped walking on two legs or when my hands became wings. One day the weight in my chest grew so heavy I had to trade it for feathers. I lifted off the ground without fanfare, without witness, just the quiet rush of air and the sudden absence of gravity.

Up here I glide.

The earth stretches beneath me like an old memory, distant and soft around the edges. Trees no longer loom, they ripple, roads no longer trap, they disappear.

People become smudges moving through their lives with an urgency that no longer belongs to me. There is no schedule in the sky, no inbox, no mirror.

I ride the warm updrafts, letting them carry me. I do not force the flight, I surrender to it, the wind does not demand explanations, it simply lifts.

In this form, I do not have to answer the hard questions, I do not have to explain the invisible weight I have carried for years, or why some days my voice cracks when I say, "I am fine." Up here I do not have to speak at all. I just am.

I drift over open fields, mountains, spines, long forgotten backroads.

My shadow follows me, silent, faithful. I forget what shame feels like. I forget the constant tallying of flaws. I forget the name I used to say when someone asked, "Who are you?" And then the light changes.

The sun dips low, bleeding across the sky in a soft golden sigh. The thermals grow weaker, the wind a little less kind. I circle once more, slower now my wings aching gently with memory. And I begin to fall.

Not in fear, but in return. My feathers melt away like old stories. My bones stretch and shift, grounding themselves. My hands come back first, fingers tingling with blood, still remembering the shape of wing beats, then breath, deep human, breathing heavy with meaning.

My feet find the earth, my skin knows gravity again.

I stand in the grass, barefoot and blinking, the sky above me still wide and indifferent. I remember everything. Not all at once but gently, like the settling of dust.

I am a person again.

But I am different now. I carry the sky in my lungs, I carry silence in my pockets. I carry, that weightless, when I was nothing but motion and light.

And maybe, just maybe, I know how to fly even when I am standing still.

What We Lost, What Remains

I still set a place for her at dinner, not out of habit, not anymore. It is an act of rebellion now, against time, against forgetting, against the slow decay of memory that everyone keeps telling me is healthy.

They do not know what true love really is.

Her name was Zoe, it still is, only now it is said in whispers, like a prayer I am no longer allowed to say out loud. She left three winters ago, it was snowing that day, the kind of snow that falls softly, like the world is trying to muffle the sound of a heart breaking. She did not scream neither did I, maybe that is what hurts the most, we said goodbye with too much silence, too much dignity. Like strangers parting after a long conversation on a train. But we were never strangers, we were everything.

She said she loved someone else. That she did not mean for it to happen, that it just did. I wanted to ask her when exactly she stopped loving me, but I was too afraid of the answer. Instead I nodded like a woman signing a contract she had not read, and I watched her walk away, her coat catching snowflakes like a dream dissolving into air.

Since then I have been walking through life like a ghost in my own story.

I get up, go to work, come home, and eat in silence. I check the door more times than I would ever admit. Just in case she changes her mind, just in case the part of her that once laughed into my neck at midnight remembers that, I am still here.

I loved her more than air, more than reason, I loved her like a religion, blindly and without limits. Every version of my future had her in it. Now the future feels like a dead language, something I knew, but can not quite understand anymore.

People tell me I should move on, I have tried, God knows I have tried. But grief is not linear, it is not tidy. It does not care about how many months have passed. It lives inside you like an echo, like a wound that never really scabs over. I hear her voice in songs, I even dream in her handwriting sometimes.

Still there is this flicker in me, a foolish, stubborn hope that maybe, one day, love will circle back. Maybe when the dust settles and life gets quiet again she will remember, maybe our souls, if not our bodies are still reaching for each other in some unseen place.

Maybe we just got the timing wrong.

Until then I will wait, not with open arms, but with an open heart. I will keep loving her even if she never returns. Because some loves do not end. They just wait for the next life or the next chance.

And maybe, just maybe she will find me there.

Pulled Back

I do not remember exactly how I got there, I remember walking in the cold, the sound of traffic beneath me like distant waves. I remember the stillness in my chest, not calm, just empty. Numb, silence the kind of silence that settles in when you have been holding too much for too long in your mind.

The bridge was just there, quite unassuming. I leaned over the edge and did not think about life or death. Just an end. The world below moved on without me. Cars, lights, people who probably had plans for the weekend. I had nothing but the weight in my bones and the noise in my head. Telling me it would be easier if I disappeared.

So I stepped over the edge.

And for the briefest moment, I felt weightless, not free, just done. Like I had finally stopped fighting. And then hands, strong real, grabbing at my coat pulling me back. A voice calm, steady, as if everything was not about to fall apart. "I have got you," he said.

I did not resist, I just collapsed, my body gave out before my mind caught up. I could not look anyone in the eye. I did not even know if I wanted to be saved. But someone thought I was worth saving.

That moment did not fix me, it did not ease the pain. But it kept me here. And staying here. And since then it has been the hardest and most important thing I have ever done. STAYING.

Recovery is not a straight line, hell it is not even easy. I still have days where the shadows return. When my chest tightens and my brain whispers lies too loud to ignore. But I also have days where I laugh until I can not breathe. I have sunrises I never would have seen. Conversations at a special place called Bridewell Gardens, a place of recovery, conversations with Paul I would never have had, things I learned from him about wildlife were amazing. I miss you Paul and I hope you have found the peace you deserved. And some special people I would never have met staff and gardeners (you know who you are).

I am still here.

Some days, I do not feel grateful for that, and that is ok. I have learned not to punish myself for having bad days, only to stay through them. To remind myself that they will pass, they always do. The trick is, to get through that day one step at a time.

I owe my life to a stranger who reached out at the right moment. But I owe it to every hard choice I have made since, to stay, to try, to heal, I am imperfect but I am still here and still trying.

Afterword for anyone who has been there.

If you are reading this and you have ever felt that pull to disappear, I want you to know something-

You are not broken.
You are not beyond saving.
You are not weak for feeling overwhelmed by pain.

You are still here, and that means there is still space for something different, even if it is just a quiet morning. Even if it is just breathing. Even if it is just not giving up today.

Please do not be afraid to ask for help. You do not have to carry everything alone, you do not have to be okay, you do not have to be ok to stay. You are worth pulling back, you are worth holding onto. Your story is not over yet.

I Am A Tear (poem)

I was born in silence
Not the peaceful kind
The kind that follows pain
The kind that lingers after words
Strike deeper than any blade

I am a tear

Not of joy, not of laughter
I was not invited, I was summoned
Called forth by something broken inside her

I slid down her cheek slowly
Clinging to skin still warm with hope
She did not brush me away, she let me fall
And the moment I touched the ground
Everything changed

You see in this world
I am not just salt and water
I am currency
I am memory
I am consequence

I am a tear

The man who caused me stood frozen
One cruel sentence, a moment of pride
Of anger, and now me
The council came
They examined me like art, like evidence
Not because I am rare
But because I am real

I carry the weight of her pain
I glitter because she did not deserve it

And for that she must pay

They say it is just
That sorrow must be counted for
She gave twenty years for me
Twenty years for one drop

She did not cry, not yet
But she will
And when she does, perhaps I will
Meet more like me
Tears with their own stories

Until then I lay here , crystalized on stone
A quiet reminder to every passerby

Think before you speak
Because when I fall
You can never take me back

I am a tear.

A Letter They Will Never Read

I do not know what I expected to feel, sitting here with this pen in my hand. Maybe some kind of release, maybe peace. But all I feel is a kind of quiet that hums beneath my ribs, heavy still. The kind of quiet you only notice when you have run out of things to say to yourself.

I do not want to make this dramatic, I am not writing this to guilt anyone or make a scene. I just need someone, anyone to just understand what it is like in my head. Maybe if you read this you will finally hear me, even if it is too late.

I have spent so long trying to be okay, trying to smile the right way. Say the right things, pretend I did not feel the things I felt. I played the part, I walked through days like they were stages, each one with new lines I had to memorize just to seem normal, just to be accepted, just to be loved.

But the truth? I always felt like a ghost standing just outside the frame of everyone else's lives.

There is this kind of loneliness that eats away at you slowly. It is not dramatic, It does not scream. It whispers, day after day. You do not matter, no one is coming for you, it just eats away at you.

I used to believe that one day someone would choose me, really choose me. Not out of pity, not because they were lonely too, but because they saw me. Because they liked what they saw, but that day never came. I thought it had but it went away quicker than it came.

Instead I became good at shrinking myself hiding behind a disguise, At not taking up space, at making myself easier to ignore it is strange how rejection stops being sharp and just becomes part of your everyday skin. I started to expect it, and worse I started to believe I deserved it. People called me a freak, so I gave them a freak. I dressed in totally black, I became that freak.

What hurts the most is not the silence, it is the pretending it does not hurt. It is smiling when someone walks past you like you were never there. It is sending messages into the void and still checking your phone knowing no one will write back, waiting days for people you love to even bother texting back. It is waking up and feeling nothing, but the weight of another day you did not ask for.

I keep hoping things will change, that I would meet someone who could sit with me in the darkness and try not to fix it, just stay, just be there. But no one ever stayed. They came close, sometimes close sometimes, close enough to touch, but never close enough to hold.

Maybe it is me, maybe I am too much or not enough or some impossible mix of both.

I do not want to die, but I do want the pain to stop. I want to be held like it matters. I want to be chosen for me. But I am tired of holding on for a future that never arrives, I am tired of being strong for everyone else while no one notices I am breaking, I am tired of pretending this is not killing me.

If you are reading this, do not remember me as a tragedy. Remember me as someone who tried. Someone who carried the weight quietly. Someone who just wanted to be seen. I did not want to go, I just did not know how to stay.

Later when they found the letter, no one spoke for a long time. I was still here, still alive.

It sat on my bed where I left it for a long time. Like a wound that would not close. The paper was worn at the edges, like it had been held a dozen times before. But I could not let it go nor destroy it for good. It is not a reminder it is part of me that tried to reach out once again. But no one listened.

Still no one listens properly, but I will try my hardest to listen to you if you ever need to reach out.

Let Them Speak

I never wanted to be in a house full of voices, but here I am.

Somedays, the voices are murmurs, like rain tapping on a window. Other days they are a storm tearing through the rooms, shouts echoing off the walls, each one demanding to be heard. I can not tell which one is me, or even if there is a me beneath all this noise.

The voices are so many, there is the calm one who tries to reason, makes lists, trying to keep me sane.

There is the angry one, sharp and biting, the voice that wants to lash out for no reason.

There is the young scared one hiding in a corner barely whispering.

There is the protector, the one who will defend until the end.

And there is the one who laughs, always laughing when all I want to do is scream.

I used to fight them and tried to silence the noise. Trying to find the real me, hiding beneath the chaos, I would sit with notebooks trying to catch a single clear thought like a butterfly. But the more I chased, the faster they scattered.

So now I try to let them speak.

I let the angry one shout at the world, even when I do not want to, trying to control his other urges to lash out.

I let the scared one curl up and stay silent for a while. I even let the laughter take over when nothing else makes sense.

Sometimes, people notice that they say I am unpredictable, scary, and dangerous. "Why can't you just be normal?" They ask. Normal is a word I do not know anymore, normal is boring.

The chaos does not just live in my head, it leaks out, spills over into conversations, into the way I move, the way I smile, or snap or just stay quiet. They even ask me who has come out today, who is speaking.

Yesterday I was in a cafe waiting for my coffee, and the

calm voice was in charge. I was polite, smiled at the barista, said, "Thank you" like a person who belonged. But then the angry voice bursts in, snapping at someone who accidentally bumped my shoulder, the calm one tried to smooth it over. But the angry one would not be ignored. I left the cafe embarrassed feeling like a stranger to myself.

And that is the truth, sometimes I do not know who I am from moment to moment. But maybe that is okay. Maybe the self is not one thing, maybe it is a crowd, a riot, A choir singing different songs at once.

I am not broken, maybe I am just many.

The Scars I Carry

There was a time I did not know how else to live.

I did not want to die, that is what people do not always understand. I just do not know how to be here in my own skin, in my own head, with all the heaviness I carried. I was drowning in silence, in sadness, in a numbness so deep it terrified me. And in that darkness, cutting became the only thing that made me feel anything at all.

The deeper the cut, the more it reminded me I was still here, that I still existed even if it was only barely. Pain for a while was the only feeling that did not lie. It became a way to take control when everything else felt completely out of it.

It was not for show, I never wanted anyone to see. I hid the wounds, wore long sleeves in the summer, learned how to smile with hollow eyes. I went through the motions while my mind was elsewhere, somewhere cold, isolated, and quiet.

I did not know how to ask for help, I did not think I deserved it.

I can not name the exact moment things started to change, maybe it was a look someone gave me that held no judgement, just concern. Maybe it was the day I put the blade down and cried for the first time instead. Maybe it was the smallest, kindest words at the right time.

You matter, you are not alone.

Healing did not come in a straight line, It still does not, there were relapses, there were moments I held pain in my hands again and had to choose. Sometimes minute by minute I let it go. But slowly I found new ways to feel, healthier ways to speak. I began to believe that I did not have to suffer to survive.

Now I look at the scars on my arms and I do not feel ashamed. I feel grateful.

Not because I am proud of the pain, but because I am proud I survived it. These scars are part of me, proof that I lived through something I did not think I would. They remind me how far I have come from the days when the only way I knew how to cope was to bleed.

Today I use that pain not to hurt myself, but to help others. I reach out to those who feel lost in the same darkness I once lived in. I sit with people who do not know how to speak their pain out loud. I listen, I do not judge, I do not try to fix. I am simply there to listen. I simply say, "I have been there, I get it, you are not alone." And I mean every word.

The scars are still here, they always will be, but now they do not define my pain, they define my strength. They remind me that even at my lowest, I choose to keep going. That even in the moments I feel like nothing, there was something, someone, inside me that refused to give up.

And now I live for that part of me. The part that survived, the part that heals, the part that reaches back for others and says-

You can Survive Too.

Journal Entry

23 March 2024

When The Storm Comes

I never hear it coming.

There is no warning, no shift in the air, no sirens blaring in my mind saying, "Hey, something's not right." It just starts quietly, so quietly, I do not even notice.

One moment I am doing something normal, making coffee, texting someone back, playing my guitar, writing songs. And then suddenly I am not there anymore. Or am I, but not fully. It is like watching myself from far away. Like I have been pushed into the back seat of my brain.

That is when the sabotage begins.

I will ruin something, say the wrong thing, cancel everything that matters to me. Sometimes I destroy what I love the most, just so I do not know how fragile it is. It always feels like survival at the time, like I am doing what I have to do. Like setting fire to my own house because something unseen is crawling up the walls.

But after I look around and nothing makes sense. My memory turns foggy, time skips like a scratched CD. I lose hours, days I will reread texts I do not remember sending. See things I have done and have no idea why.

It is terrifying.

There is this weird, weightless feeling that comes with it, like being underwater or floating in space. I can hear myself talking, but I do not feel attached to it. My limbs move, but they do not feel like mine. I see my face in the mirror and it does not look familiar. Like I am borrowing someone else,s body, someone else,s name.

Sometimes I cry, sometimes I just go completely blank. Like my brain has pulled the plug on me to stop the system from over heating. And then just like that it is over.

The world keeps spinning, and I am standing in the wreckage, exhausted, confused, ashamed. Trying to remember how it started, trying to remember, understand how I lost control so fast and why. I never saw the edge before I fell.

People think you feel a mental health crisis coming, that there is a clear start, a dramatic middle, and a resolution. But this is not like that, this is a silent land slide. It happens underneath me, and by the time I notice, I have already fallen.

And afterwards, I am left to pick up the pieces of whatever damage I did. I try to explain it sometimes, but how do you explain something you do not even remember clearly? How do you take responsibility for a version of yourself you barely recognise? I hate that part, the not knowing, the blank spaces in the story. The fear that I will do it again and not even realize I am doing it.

Sometimes I wish I could leave a note for myself. Something like, "Hey, it is happening again. Breathe, do not burn it down this time."

But it never works like that.

All I can do is sit here afterward in the quiet exhausted trying to come back into my body, trying to trust my mind again. Trying to stay.

End Note:

I do not have a perfect ending for this, there is no clear lesson tied up in a bow. Just this I am still here, do not know how, but I still am. Still learning to live with a brain that sometimes turns against me. Still finding my way back when I disappear. Still trying to hold onto parts of me that survive the storm.

If you have felt like this too, the silence before the chaos during the hollow. You are not alone. We may forget how we got lost, confused when we wake up in hospital. But we can still find our way back. Even if it is slow, even if we have to do it more than once.

Even if we have to do it every damn day.

We will find our way back.

Empire Above The Clouds (Part One)

I do not remember the exact moment it happened. No crashing sounds, no cinematic gasp for air, just a strange calm. Like slipping beneath the surface of warm water and forgetting to be afraid. The noise of the world dimmed, softened into something almost gentle. Time thinned out, stretched like the space between heartbeats. I had taken too many pills, enough to silence the chaos inside me, but instead of darkness there was light and something more than light. A vastness, stillness and somewhere above me, or maybe inside me. I felt the pull of something enormous. Like an empire waiting in the clouds.

I was not floating, not exactly. More like suspended, no weight, no ground, no sky. Just a place between the air if that is what it was, smelled like nothing but not in an empty way, in a pure way. It was quiet too, the kind of quiet that makes you realize how loud life always is.

Shapes started to form around me. Not solid, not even clearly visible, but it felt like I was not alone.

The first figure I saw was my grandmother, she had been gone for years, but there she was. Not the way I remembered her at the end, weak and small in a hospital bed, but as she used to be, tall, strong, laughing with her whole chest. She did not speak but her presence wrapped around me like a warm blanket you forgot existed.

I wanted to run to her but I could not move. Or maybe I did not need to, she was already with me.

More figures came, emerging like smoke taking shape. A friend (Anne) from my childhood who I lost as an 18 year old. My aunt who was always there for me, my mum who I miss so much, my sister. People I had loved, people I had lost, they did not say anything either. Just stood there reaching out to me, waiting, watchful, tender, loving.

I thought I should be afraid, but I was not, then I saw it.

Above us above even them was something so huge it

made my chest ache to look at it. Towers of light, architecture made of clouds and memory. An empire so tall it stretched into forever. And far below barely visible through the shifting mists, was something else, fire maybe movement. A city of shadows, something older than time or sorrow.

Heaven above hell below.

And I am stuck in between.

Empire Above The Clouds (Part Two)

They did not speak, not in the way people do. But I felt them. Felt their feelings, like waves passing through me. Sadness, yes but not for me, for what I had carried. For how heavy the years had been. For how close I came to never returning.

My Grandmother reached out not her hand but something deeper. And suddenly I was awash in memories. Not the big ones, not birthdays or funerals. The small ones her singing to herself and washing dishes. The way she squeezed my shoulder when she knew I was lying. Her laugh when something was truly stupidly funny, I felt it all, and in that moment. I wondered if maybe this was what heaven really was, not a place but a remembering, a reunion.

But something in me recoiled. Not because I did not want to believe it, because I did too much.

I looked up again at the city of light. It shimmered impossibly tall, like the world had grown teeth made of glass. I wanted it to be real, I wanted to belong there. But doubt crawled in like smoke under a door. Was this a glimpse of the afterlife? Or just my brain burning through its last electricity, projecting comfort on a dying screen.

If heaven was real, did that mean hell was too? I looked down.

The city below flickered, not fire, not entirely. Motion faces in the dark. Buildings hunched like predators, a place where regrets walked on two legs and never stopped whispering.

Some part of me wondered if I had gone just a little further, is that where I have ended up?

I turned to the faces around me, my friend who took her own life at eighteen. My aunt who was always there for me, my grandmother and my mum who I had loved so much. I wanted to ask them, was I meant to die? Were you waiting for me? But no words came. Only a feeling, rising slow and steady like the tide.

Not yet it said.

You are not done.

And then I felt it. The weight of my body, the sting of pain creeping back into my limbs, the cold taste of air as something forced its way into my lungs. A distant beeping, metal, voices, panic. I was being pulled back.

Empire Above The Clouds (Part Three)

Coming back did not feel like waking up. It felt like falling.

Hard, slow, and wrong like being dragged out of warmth into ice. I opened my eyes and saw light, but not the empire above the clouds. Fluorescent, buzzing sterile light. The ceiling of a hospital. The sharp, rhythmic beep of a machine tracking what was left of me. My mouth was dry, my arms were heavy, I could not move at first and part of me did not want to.

A nurse was saying my name, gently like she was trying not to scare me.

"You are ok, you are safe, you are here," but I was not sure where there was any more.

I did not cry, not right away, the calm had not left me completely, but it had changed. It was no longer peaceful, it was hollow, like something had been ripped from me in that in-between place. Something I almost understood. The doctors asked questions, and so did my family. I nodded, lied, stayed silent where I could. No one really knew what to say, and neither did I, how do you tell someone you saw the shape of forever? How do you explain a place that might have been heaven (when you do not believe) or just the flicker of your subconscious begging you not to go?

I kept seeing my friend's face (Anne came back with me) not the way she looked at me in real life, but the version I saw there, whole, warm, real. Her silence haunted me more than anything. Not because it was cold, but because it was kind she understood me. And because she told me not to stay. She did not tell me it was ok to come with her, she let me choose.

And I did not choose anything, I just woke up.

For days, it felt like I was walking around in two worlds. This one full of hate, noise and clocks, and people asking me how I was doing with eyes that did not really want the truth. And the other, the space between sky and earth, light and fire, memory and imagination was it real?

Was I dying or just dreaming, just wanting to be where I knew people loved me?

I do not know.

I still do not know.

But I know what I felt. I know what I saw, I know that for a few moments. I stood between two empires, one above the clouds, and one below the ground, and that something or someone sent me back.

Maybe it was love.

Maybe it was god.

Maybe it was just my own mind refusing to let go of a world I had not finished understanding.

Closing Reflection:

I have tried to explain it, once or twice, not the pills, not the hospital, but the other part. In between, most people nod politely, some change the subject, some just do not listen, but hey I am used to that, or not hence why I am where I am. A few listen too closely like they are afraid. I might tell them something that makes their own walls crack.

I get it we all want to believe in something, but we are scared of what belief really costs. That if we admit there might be more, we also have to admit we do not know what that, MORE, is or what it asks of us.

Since that day I have stopped trying to work it out.

I do not know if there is a heaven or hell, maybe we build them ourselves. Maybe they are waiting just out of reach, shaped by what we carry in our hearts. Maybe the empire above the clouds is real, and maybe I saw it because some part of me needed it to be. Maybe that's all belief ever is, reaching for something bigger than our pain, hoping it reaches back.

But here is what I believe.

Something caught me.

Whether it was love, or luck or a grandmother's silent refusal to let me go, I do not know. But I came back and that has to mean something.

Not that I am cured. Not that the dark does not still visit sometimes. But now when it does I remember that quiet, that vastness, that moment when I stood on the edge of eternity and was told in no uncertain terms.

Not yet.

So I stay, I try, I breathe.

And when the sky is heavy with clouds, I look up, not for answers, but for the memory of that empire, still waiting somewhere above all of this.

Still Breathing

Some mornings, I wake up and forget where I am, not in space but in time. For a split second I still expect to feel her beside me. Her warmth, the familiar weight of her presence. The comfort of knowing I was loved.

But then it comes back to me like a knife through the fog, She's gone.

And she is not just gone, she is with someone else now.

That thought does not sting, it burns.

It burns because I remember everything, how she used to look at me, how she laughed like I was the funniest person alive, how I thought she was mine forever. But forever is not a promise, it is a memory now.

And still the world moves like nothing's changed.

People smile at me in passing, I nod back and say, "I am good," because it is easier than the truth, but inside, there is still this silence, heavy and echoing like something screaming underwater.

I walk through my days on autopilot, work, eat, sleep, repeat. I meet new people. Sometimes I shake hands, make small talk but they do not see it. They do not see the war inside me.

Depression is not loud, it is not crying all the time, it's forgetting how to feel joy. It is sitting in a room full of people and feeling utterly alone. It is brushing your teeth and feeling like you have run a marathon. It is missing someone who is still alive, but not yours anymore.

And then there's the trauma, the flashbacks, the way certain places, smell or songs bring everything crashing back. Some nights, sleep never comes, other nights I pray not to wake up. But I always wake up. And that some days is the hardest part. Waking up.

I miss the versions of me who used to believe in things in love, in trust, in the future. Now I just need to survive the day. Sometimes that is enough, other times it is not.

But I have learned to count victories now, not in milestones, but in moments.

And you can too.

Getting out of bed when I do not want to, letting the sun touch my face, drinking water, texting someone back, letting myself cry instead of holding it in. letting myself feel even when it hurts like hell.

And once in a while, rarely, but still I laugh, a real laugh, surprising, foreign but mine. And for a second, I think maybe I am still here somewhere.

I do not know when things will get better. I do not know if I will ever love someone like I loved her. But I do know this.

I am still here, people set out to ruin my relationship. They succeeded, but I am still here, still breathing, still trying.

And maybe that is what strength really is, not pretending you are fine, but choosing to stay when every part of you wants to disappear.

So I keep going, not for her, not for anyone else.

But For Me.

For the version of me that is still lost, still healing, but not done yet. Because somewhere down this road, there is peace, maybe even happiness again. Not the same as before, but something new.

And when I find it, if I find it, I will think it was worth it, was worth every step through the dark.

Puzzle Head

I imagine my brain as a jigsaw puzzle.

Not a shiny 500 piece set from a toy shop, with smiling landscapes or sleepy kittens. No mine is a weather worn heap dumped out on the floor with no box, no picture, and no instructions. The kind you find at the bottom of a charity bin. Warped by damp, some corners chewed others missing altogether.

And still I try to put it together.

Some pieces shine, fragments of laughter, a flicker of calm, a moment of connection. But most are dull, cracked or feel like they belong to someone else entirely.

There are blank spots, not just metaphorical ones. I mean hours and days go missing, I come to find notes in my own hand writing. Sent messages I do not remember typing. Conversations that drift around me like echoes I never said. People look at me with an expression, I do not understand and I realise I have said something, or done something in the missing time.

I live in these absences, trying to make sense of actions that leave no trace in my memory, only in other people's eyes.

Doctors say things like dissociation or episodes, or neurodivergence. I nod like they have given me puzzle pieces. But their words are shapes without colour, they do not really fit, not really.

Sometimes I imagine what the picture would look like, if I ever finished the puzzle. A face, a landscape, a childhood memory before the cracks began. Hell my teenage years, lots of gaps there. Maybe something softer, maybe nothing at all, maybe the picture was never printed, maybe I am building something that does not have a final image. Only an endless process of trial and error.

I spend most days hunting for corners, anchors, and simple routines. The smell of coffee in the morning, the sound of my neighbours banging doors. A voice message from a friend checking in, gently reminding me I exist.

Those are the pieces I start with, the ones I press into the board and pray they will hold steady.

But some days the pieces do not fit, my hands shake, my thoughts scatter. I forget how to sleep or why I started cleaning or whether I have eaten. I speak in sentences that lose their endings. I sit in the dark even if the light is on, overwhelmed by a thousand floating shapes, unsure which ones belong now. Hell sometimes I do not know what is real, or if I am alive or dead.

I have learned not to fight the confusion too hard. It only makes the puzzle angrier. Instead I breathe, I say, "Okay this is what today looks like" and I try to find just one piece to hold onto.

Sometimes I find others like me, people with their own unfinished puzzles. They understand the silence, the shame, the way you can look completely fine while falling apart in twelve invisible places.

We exchange pieces, not to complete each other, but to feel a little less alone in the chaos.

And slowly, slowly I have learned that this puzzle might never be done. That the point is not completion, but presence. That maybe healing is not solving, but simply staying with myself, even when the image makes no sense.

Because even if the picture is crooked, incomplete, and full of gaps.

It is mine and the others that share my mind. My fragile mind.

And I am still building the puzzle in my head.

Edges Of Me

Some mornings I wake up feeling like a thousand wires are tangled beneath my skin. Too tight, too loud, it is like I have woken up inside a body that does not fit right. I stretch my hand toward the phone to check the messages, nothing, no reply, even though I can see they have read mine.

My stomach drops, my mind goes straight to the worse case scenario. Maybe they are ignoring me, maybe they are done, maybe I said too much, or not enough.

By the time I brush my teeth, I have imagined at least five versions of them leaving me, blocking me, hating me, I do not even know what is real anymore. All I know is that I feel like I might die from the ache in my chest. If they do not reply.

Then they do.

A heart emoji, three words, *Sorry, just busy.*

And just like that I am flying. The relief floods in so fast I could cry. I love them, I love everyone, I am ok again. I almost laughed at myself, god I was being so dramatic.

But deep down, I know this is going to happen again. Probably tomorrow.

That is what it is like living in my skin, this is the rollercoaster I can not get off. This is BPD/EUPD (Borderline personality disorder/Emotional Unstable Personality Disorder.) Or whatever the professionals want to call it. I call it hell, I call it home. It is the only way I have ever known how to feel.

I met her nearly 20 years ago. Let's just call her A. She made me feel seen in a way that no one had before. She looked at me like I was a whole person, not just a list of symptoms. I told her everything too soon but I could not help it. I needed her to know me all of me, I wanted to merge with her, become one person. That is how it feels with people I love, like I do not know where I end and they begin.

She texted me every single day, and I lived for it.

I knew it was not normal, I knew I was depending on her too

much. But logic does not mean anything when your emotions hit you like a hurricane. When she did not message I felt abandoned, betrayed, like I was not real anymore. I spiraled, I would panic, send ten messages in a row. Then I would delete them all, then I would send one to say, "I am sorry, ignore me, I am just being stupid." Then I would hate her for not understanding. And then I would hate myself for needing her.

The truth is I could never hate her, and I will always need her.

She told me once, "I am not going anywhere."

That was a lie, maybe not on purpose, but still.

The last time we spoke, I accused her of being fake, a liar, a cheat, I told her she used me. I said horrible things, words like knives, because I needed her to feel what I was feeling. I needed her to stay, or at least react. She did not, she went quiet.

Now all I have is screenshots of the truth, and an overanalyzed message.

Sometimes I feel like a puppet on strings I did not choose.

Someone looks at me the wrong way and my whole body flinches. A sharp tone and I am crying, a compliment and I love you. A joke that hits to close I hate you.

People think I am manipulative, I get it, but the truth is I am desperate, I am terrified, I do not know how to live in this world without begging for love in ways that did not make sense. And the worst part? I do not even know who I am. My sense of self is like fog, I think I see it, but when I reach for it, it slips away.

One day I want to be an artist, the next a nurse, the next I want to disappear completely. I look in the mirror and I do not recognize the person staring back. I try on personalities like outfits, hoping one might finally fit.

But they never do.

Last night I had a moment, I was sitting on the bathroom floor cold under my thighs, staring at a line of texts I never sent. I felt empty, not sad, not angry, just gone like someone had turned off the lights inside me. That is what no one talks about, the quiet after the storm, the numbness. It is like being dead but still breathing.

I stared at the razor in the drawer for a long time.

I did not touch it, not because I did not want to, I just did not move, sometimes the nothingness is scarier than the pain. Today I went for a walk, just around the block. There was this little kid holding her mum's hand swinging it back and forth, skipping along like life was just one long playground. I do not remember ever feeling like that. Not really I have always felt too much or not enough.

Still I watched her smile, and for a second I wondered what it would be like to live without constant fear, without the need for someone else to fill the gaps inside me. What would it be like to just be?

I do not know, but I want to, even just for a moment.

If you are reading this and any of this sounds familiar, like looking into a mirror you did not know existed, I want to tell you something.

You are not crazy.
You are not broken.
You are not a burden.

I know it feels like you are too much, or that you will never be enough. But you are here. And that means something that means everything.

People do not see what it costs us just to exist some days, to fight the voices that tell us we are unloveable, or disgusting, or dangerous. People think we are dramatic or manipulative or unstable, they do not see the war inside, the aching, the desperate hope for connection. The soft parts of us that believe someone might stay.

I am not fixed, I still fall apart, I still send the text then delete it. I still cry over things I cannot explain. I still miss people who hurt me, I still love people who left. I am still learning how to be alone without falling into pieces.

But I am her.

And that counts for something.

AUTHOR NOTES:

If any part of this felt familiar, if you saw yourself in these words, I want you to know you are not alone. Living with BPD/EUPD is not easy. The emotions, the fear, the intensity, the emptiness. It can feel overwhelming. But help exists, and healing is possible. Please reach out.

Talk to someone you trust, a friend, a therapist, a crisis line. You do not have to carry this by yourself. You are not a burden, there are people who want to understand you. People who want to walk alongside you, I want to walk alongside you. Even when you feel unlovable, there are people there.

Asking for help is not a weakness, in fact it is a kind of courage most people will never understand.

You deserve support.
You deserve peace.
You deserve to stay.

From Shadow To Sunlight

I lived in the quiet corners of the world.

Not the world everyone else moved through, the one with chatter, with sunlight and smiles and the hum of life, but a smaller, stiller one. One made of closed curtains, soft footsteps, and a silence so thick I could almost wrap it around myself like a blanket. My phone gathered dust, my diary still stayed empty. Days came and went like waves that barely touched the shores.

To others, I was just quiet, private, maybe even introverted. But behind closed doors, fear was the loudest sound. I was afraid to say the wrong thing, afraid to go out and be seen. Afraid of the world's gaze and of its indifference, I avoided phone calls, I avoided mirrors (still do) I avoided life. Even small tasks like, going to the shop, replying to a message. It felt like walking through thick fog, never sure what or who I would bump into, or if I would find my way back.

Isolation did not come all at once, it was slow, subtle at first, it felt like rest, peace, then comfort, then safety and then one day, I realised I was not resting, I was hiding.

The shadows were my sanctuary, but they were also my cage.

One morning I noticed a sliver of light on the wall, it came through a gap in the curtains I had not closed properly the night before. It lit up a dusty shelf and a crumpled jumper I had not worn in months. I stared at it for a long time. There was something about it, simple, quiet, certain. Like it did not need me to do anything. It just was, I did not touch the curtain, I let the light stay.

That was the first crack.

A week later, I opened the window, it sounded small but my hand shook on the latch. I half expected the outside world to rush in and demand something of me, but all that came was a breeze, cool, fresh, kind, I leaned toward it, letting it run across my skin.

My shoulders dropped. My jaw was unclenched. The next week, I stood by the door, the week after that I stepped outside, just a foot, then back in that was enough.

There was no great moment. No dramatic epiphany. Just a string of tiny braveries. Healing did not look like I thought it would. It was not fireworks or instant peace. It was awkward first steps, forced smiles, crying for no reason and then laughing because I was crying. It was journaling in half sentences and deleting messages before I sent them, and then one day, actually sending one.

It was rediscovering music I used to love, cooking something simple, walking to the end of the street without headphones in, just listening, noticing, being.

Sometimes I still felt the pull of the shadows, I still do, but the sun started to feel more like home.

Now I sit in a park not far from my home, it is late afternoon and golden light filters through the trees. Children's laughter rings in the air. Somewhere someone is playing a guitar. A breeze dances across the grass and touches my face.

I am not healed in the way stories often promise, I am healing though slowly which is harder. Which is real.

I speak more freely now. I make mistakes, I try again, the fear still whispers but it no longer controls the volume. And when I feel it creeping back the shadows, the silence. I remember the sunlight, I remember the sunlight, I remember how it first found me, even when I was not looking.

So I keep going, one breath, one step, one sliver of light at a time.

But I do now, step out of the shadows and into the sunlight.

Just for your breath, open your eyes step outside, one step at a time.

I know you can do it, and I will do it with you.

If You Cant Hear me, You Are Not Listening (poem)

Do not say I am quiet.
Do not say I have changed.
I have been screaming in silence.
While you rearranged.
The truth to suit.
What you wanted to see.
But you have never once really looked at me.

I speak in storms, I bleed in light.
I have whispered hope.
Through sleepless nights.
But your ears are locked.
To what you do not like.
And you call me distant.
When I am just tired of the fight.

You hear the words.
You wish I had to say.
The soft, the safe.
The fade away.
But when I speak fire.
You flinch and flee.
As if honesty is cruelty.
When it is not quite.
Not pretty, not sweet.

You ask, "Why did you not tell me?"
I did.
You just were not there to hear it.
Not really, Not fully.
Not with this kind of care.
That makes someone feel seen.

So no.

It is not that I am not speaking.
It is not that I am not here.
It is that you stopped listening.
Long before.
I disappeared.

The Loneliest Place

People think the loneliest is about being alone, an empty room, a quiet weekend, no one texting back. But the loneliest place I have ever been is inside my own head.

It does not matter how many people are around me. I can be at a birthday party, a cafe, even surrounded by close friends. I can laugh, make conversation, play along, and still feel like I am not really there, like I am watching myself through a screen. Stuck behind glass no one else can see through.

It starts quietly. A voice in my mind, soft but certain, "You do not belong here."

At first, I ignore it, smile, nod, pretend I am fine. But the voice does not go away, it grows.

They are just being polite, they do not actually like you. You are ruining the vibe. You sound weird, why did you say that?

Then my heart starts to race. My chest tightens, everyone's voices around me blur together, the laughter, the conversations, even the music. It all turns into static. But somehow, it still feels like they are all talking about me. I know they are not, but it feels like they are.

That is when I start acting out of character, I try too hard to be funny, say something stupid, something that is not really me. Just whatever I think will make people keep me in the room.

And when it lands wrong, which it usually does, I retreat, quiet down, shrink into my seat. I pull out my phone to fake a text. Say I am tired. Say I have got something early tomorrow, and I leave,

But the worst part comes after.

I walk home in silence. But my mind does not stop, it replays everything in brutal detail. The faces people made, the way someone turned away mid sentence. The look I imagined in someone's eyes. It does not matter if it really happened, my brain fills in the blanks with the worst possible answers.

They are tired of you.

They talk about you when you are not there.
They wish you would just stop showing up.

That is when loneliness really hits, not because I was alone, but because I was still with people and still felt completely unseen. Like I was shouting in a crowded room and no one could hear me. Or worse, they could, and chose not to.

Anxiety turns everything into a threat, every text, every silence, every smile that does not quite reach someone's eyes. It builds this false reality that feels truer than anything real. And that is what makes it isolating. Because when your mind becomes the enemy, there is no safe place to go, not even inside yourself.

And you start to pull back, you stop texting first, you cancel plans, you disappear, not because you do not want a connection but because you have convinced yourself you do not deserve it. That you are the problem, your presence is a burden.

That is the loneliest place, not the empty room, but the full one, When you are surrounded by people, and the only thing louder than their laughter is the voice inside your own head, telling you that you are alone anyway.

I am still learning how to fight that voice. Some days I win, some days I do not, but I am trying. Because deep down, I know I want to be seen, heard, listened to, understood. And maybe, just maybe, I am not alone. Not as alone as I think.

The Loneliest Place 2 (Their Voice)

I have noticed they have gone quiet again.

Not the kind of quiet that just means tired. I have learned to tell the difference, this quiet has weight to it, like something heavy pressing down on them, like they folding into themselves, layer by layer. And every time it happens, I wonder if I did something wrong. Or if I should have said something wrong, or if I am saying too much now.

They do not reply to texts, they cancel plans at the last minute. When we do talk it is surface level, small talk with a nervous smile. But I can see it in their eyes, the way they look somewhere else when I ask if they are okay, the way they say, "I am just tired," a little too quickly.

I know they are hurting, I just do not know how to reach them. I have tried everything I can think of. I have the check in texts, I have offered to come over, I have left space, I have been patient. But nothing seems to get through. And I do not want to push them further away. I am scared of saying the wrong thing, or worse nothing at all.

Sometimes I sit with my phone in my hand, rereading our last conversation. Wondering if I missed a sign, wishing I had the right words to make them feel less alone. But I do not, I never do.

And that is the hardest part, loving someone who feels unreachable, watching them drift further inside themselves, while you are standing on the outside yelling their name but getting no answer. But I am not going anywhere, even if they pull away, even if they cannot pull away, even if they can not, or say what is wrong. Even if they do not reply for days, because even if I can not fix it, I want them to know, someone sees them, someone cares even in the quiet.

(Back to me, a small step)

I saw the message today, the one I had been ignoring, it just said, *I am here when you are ready, I care, that's all.*

I read it three times, They did not ask anything of me, They did not try to fix me, It just was there.

For a moment the noise inside me eased, not completely, but just enough to breathe. And something in me whispered, maybe you are not alone as you think.

My fingers hovered over the key pad. I did not know what to say, but I replied, *Hey, I do not know how to talk about it, but thank you,* I hit send.

It was not a fix, It was not a cure, but it was something.

Sometimes the smallest message can echo the loudest inside a lonely mind.

When Silence Speaks Louder Than Words

Some days I do not need grand gestures, or long conversations. I just need someone to ask how I am really doing, and actually wait for the answer. Not just the, "I am fine," answer. The true answer, the one behind my eyes, the one I am afraid to say out loud, because I have learned that most people do not want to hear it, or just do not listen.

I have had moments, quiet aching moments. Where I have asked for something simple, a message back, a check in, a little effort. And when it does not come it does not just feel like forgetfulness. It feels like I do not matter.

That is the part of me that hurts the most.

It is not that people are cruel, it is just that they are careless in ways that cut deeper than they know.

I do not want to be high maintenance. I do not want to be a burden. So I shrink myself down into something easier to hold. I silence my needs, convince myself I am over reacting and smile when it is the last thing I feel like doing.

But inside it is exhausting.

When I finally speak up, ask for something small, something that might help, I notice how often it is met with silence, delay or a quick change of subject. That is when the real loneliness sets in, not because I am physically alone, but because I know people do not listen. And it makes me feel emotionally invisible.

And one of the hardest things is when I share a piece of myself, maybe something I wrote, something honest and raw, and I ask someone to read it. That moment is me reaching out, opening a door, trusting them with something deeply personal. But then they do not read it, or they say they will but never do.

Days pass and nothing.

And I know it sounds small, doesn't it? But it breaks something inside me every time. Because what I wrote was not just words, it was a piece of me. A way of saying, "This is how I feel, but I do not know how else to show you".

When it is ignored, it feels like I am being ignored, and then that is when I spiral, I question if I am too much, if I expect too much, or if I should just stop asking at all.

The truth is, when someone takes the time to read what I wrote, really read it, and feel it, I feel like someone has seen me. I feel heard without having to raise my voice. And that feeling is rare, but it stays with me.

I have learned to carry a lot on my own. I am strong because I had no other choice, but I never wanted to be strong just to survive the people who could not or would not show up for me.

Sometimes I do not need anyone to fix anything. I just need to feel like I matter enough for someone to really care. To listen without trying to change the subject. To hear the pause in my voice and ask, "Are you sure?"

To remember the things I said, even when I pretend they are not important.

Because they were, they are important.

If someone like me is in your life, someone quiet, who checks in, who smiles even when their eyes look tired, do not just assume they are okay, just because they are not falling apart in front of you.

LISTEN CLOSER

Sometimes our pain is subtle, sometimes our needs are whispered. And sometimes all it takes to save someone is to notice when they are slipping and say, "I see you, I hear you, I am here."

A Note To Those Who Care

This is not about blame, this is not about understanding. I am not writing this to make anyone feel guilty. I am writing it because sometimes, I do not know how else to say what is in my heart.

If you have ever wondered how to be there for me, or someone like me, start small.

Read the things I share with you, even if they are hard. Even if you do not know what to say afterward. Ask twice when I say I am fine, show up in small quiet ways. And most of all, try to remember that just because I carry it well does not mean it is not heavy.

Your care, your attention, your effort, it matters more than you know. And sometimes it is the difference between feeling invisible and feeling human.

"All I ever wanted was to be heard."

A Song No One Will Hear (But Me)

Some nights, I do not know if I exist or if I am just passing through a world that stopped seeing me a long time ago.

There is a special kind of silence that comes with feeling alone, not the peaceful kind, not the people who write about when they want to sound poetic. This silence crushes you, it wraps around your ribs and whispers, "You are nothing" and some nights I believe it.

I had been staring at the wall for hours, the guitar leaned against the corner, collecting dust like it had given up on me too. I used to play everyday, I used to think music could save me. But lately, nothing could. Still something inside me stirred, a raw kind of ache that did not want to be quiet any more. It was not hope it was desperation, and sometimes that is where the best songs begin.

So I picked up the guitar, plugged it into my amp, strings stiff under my fingers, I did not warm up, hell I did not even tune the guitar, I just played.

One chord., then another. It did not sound good, but it sounded right that comes from matching the noise inside your head. I did not really write the lyrics, not really. They just fell out.

I scream into silence, and it answers me back
With echoes of all the things I lack.

That line did not come from thinking, it came from a place deeper than thought. That is how it usually starts. One line that punches you in the chest, that first truth opens the flood. I kept going, I let the words trip over themselves, I did not worry about rhyme or structure. It was painful just trying to be heard.

I walk through crowds like I am already gone
A ghost humming verses no one hears
And no one wants.

I paused, I felt something hot rise in my throat. I was not

crying, not really, but that line cracked me open. It was ugly, and it was real, and that is the thing. Good songs are not always beautiful. Sometimes they are just honest.

I sat in it for a while, staring at the page, fingers still on the string. And that is the hardest part, when the initial burst fades, and you have to build something out of it.

So I looked back at the words, I asked myself that question that always comes next.

What am I really trying to say?
What am I afraid to say?

That is where the chorus comes from.
But I sing anyway.

In a room no one is in.
Just to hear myself echo again.

That line felt like truth and surrender at the same time. It was a confession, I did not want to be famous, I did not want to be heard by millions. I just wanted proof my voice existed.

I kept writing, verse after verse. Not to make a hit, not to feel better, just to get it out. People think song writing is magic, sometimes it is, but most times, it is just bleeding carefully turning chaos into rhythm. Pain into melody, loneliness into something you can play back and say, "This is what it feels like inside my head."

When the song was finished, I did not smile, I did not feel proud, but I felt something I had not felt in weeks. REAL.

I recorded it in my studio, not because I wanted anyone to hear it. But because maybe someday I will need to hear it again. To remember that I made something out of the darkest part of myself.

And maybe just maybe, someone out there will hear it and whisper, "Me too,"

The song title, 'Echo,' again inspired this story. So I decided to include the lyrics in this book.

Echo Again (Song)

Verse 1
I scream into silence, and it answers me back.
With echos of all the things I lack
I pace this room like I am under attack
But no one sees the weight on my back.
I am a shadow under neon lights
A whisper trapped in sleepless nights
Trying to breathe through broken might
Wishing someone knew how to fight.

Pre Chorus
But the walls do not talk
They just stare
And I wonder if I am even there.

Chorus
But I sing anyway
In a room no one is in
Just to hear myself
Echo again
If these chords collapse
And my voice wears thin
At least I will know I tried
To echo again

Verse 2
My fingers shake on these rusted strings
But they still remember how truth stings
I bleed in lines, I don't even mean
Till the pain starts to sound like
Something clean
There is no one hear, but I still perform
To the silence that feels like a thunderstorm
This song is not pretty, it is barely warm
But it is mine, and that is the form

Pre chorus (repeats)

Chorus (repeats)

Bridge
I am not asking for a stage
Not begging for applause
Just a moment in the dark
Where i do not feel lost
Let this song be a flare
Fired into the sky
For the ones like me
Who dont know why

Final (chorus)

Outro
So I will play
Till the dark fades
One note
One breath
One day

Not the best lyrics I have done but these are lyrics from true feelings.

From The Inside Out

Part 1- The Daily Shadow

Some mornings, I did not wake up, I resurfaced. Not into light or clarity, but into a heavy shapeless weight that settled across my chest, before I even opened my eyes. I would lie there, staring at the ceiling or the wall or nothing at all, trying to gather the will to move, not to run a marathon, just to sit up, just to brush my teeth, just to exist.

It is strange how invisible depression can be. On the outside I might have looked okay, or maybe tired, quiet. But inside everything felt muted, like I was underwater every sound, every word, every face seemed far away. I answered messages with emojis and empty phrases, and I smiled at work. I said, *I was just tired,* more times than I could count. But really I was unraveling. Some days I just sat in my room and cried until I could not cry anymore. I did not know what triggered it, sometimes it was a memory, sometimes just the silence, but the pain felt overwhelming. I remember thinking, I have lost everything, not just the one I loved, opportunities, parts of myself, the joy, the hope, the version of me that could look forward to anything. It was like I had become a ghost in my own life.

The hardest part was not even the sadness. It was the nothing, the flat endless emptiness that replaced everything I used to enjoy. Music did not move me, food tasted well tasteless. Conversations felt like performances, I stopped making plans, I stopped dreaming, I stopped caring. Some days I even stopped showering. Not because I wanted to be that way, but because the energy it took to care felt impossible.

And the guilt, that was the echo that followed me everywhere. I knew people had it worse, I knew I should be grateful. I know others loved me, but depression does not care about logic, it lies, it whispers that you are a burden, that you are weak, that you are broken beyond repair. And eventually I started to believe it.

From The Inside Out

Part 2- The Loneliness And The Emptiness

Depression has a way of convincing you that you are completely alone, even when you are not. I could be in a room full of people and still feel like I was locked behind a glass wall. I could hear the laughter, the conversation, the life happening around me, but I could not feel any of it. I was disconnected, watching, nodding, pretending, but never really there.

That kind of loneliness is more than just being alone, it is feeling unseen, unheard, untouched by anything that used to matter. Even when someone asked, "Are you okay?" I could not bring myself to answer honestly. What would I say? That I felt empty? That I cried until I fell asleep and woke up really tired? That even when I smiled, I felt like I was lying? There were times when I reached out, I tried to explain what was wrong, tried to put the pain into words, but no one truly listened. Some changed the subject, others told me to, "Stay strong," or, "Just try to be more positive." and some did not say anything at all. I know they probably meant well, but it made me feel even more alone, like my pain was not valid, like I was being too dramatic, or worse like I did not matter. That silence after opening up, it hurt more than staying quiet ever did.

So eventually I stopped trying, I kept it all inside, like a secret I was ashamed to carry. I did not want to be a burden, I did not want to be too much. I stopped replying, I stopped reaching out, I stopped showing up, in texts, in conversations, in life. And no one really noticed, or at least that's what it felt like.

The emptiness became familiar, like a cold room I could not leave. And the scariest part was, after a while I stopped wanting to. I did not believe things could get better. I thought this was just who I was now, someone who just survived the day. Not someone who lived it.

From The Inside Out

Part 3- The First Cracks Of Life

For a long time I believed it was my fault, the pain, the silence, the way people pulled away or did not listen. I thought maybe I was too much. Maybe I did not know how to explain things right. Maybe it was not worth the effort.

But eventually something shifted. It did not happen in a single moment, it was slow, like light leaking through a crack in a closed door. At first I barely noticed it, but over time I began to realize, the problem was not me. It was the way people responded, it was the way some stuck their nose in without ever truly listening. The way they offered opinions instead of support, judgement instead of compassion. I was hurting and instead of holding space for me, they tried to fix me, or worse silence me. That clarity did not fix everything, but it gave me something I had not felt in a long time, strength.

I started to understand that I was not broken, I was human, I was going through something deeply painful, and I needed connection, not correction. I did not need someone to save me. I just needed someone to sit with me in the dark and say, "I see you, I hear you, you are not alone."

Bit by bit, I started to do that for myself, I gave myself permission to feel, to rest, to not be okay. And little things started to help, even if just for a moment. A quiet walk, a song I used to love, writing down what I could not say out loud (my feelings). Eventually, I found support in people who got it, who walked through the same darkness and did not try to drag me out, but simply walked alongside me.

It was still hard, some days, it still is. But there was hope now, not loud or dramatic. But real and that changed everything.

From The Inside Out

Part 4- Finding Purpose In Pain

As I started to heal, something inside me changed. The pain did not vanish, but it started to take on meaning. I had walked through something many people never talk about, and I was still here, still breathing, still trying. And that began to feel like something I could offer to others.

I did not want anyone else to feel the way I had, lost, dismissed, invisible. I knew what it was like to cry alone in a room full of memories, to reach out and be met with silence, to believe the darkness would never end.

That kind of pain leaves behind a deep understanding. And with time, that understanding turned into purpose.

It is now my goal with this deep understanding to become a peer support worker. I am not there yet but I will be. Because I know firsthand how much it means just to have someone who gets it. Someone who does need you to explain, who does not try to fix you, but who simply sits beside you and says, "You are not broken, you are not alone, I have been there too."

I want to be that person, not because I have all the answers (far from it), but because I have lived the questions. I know how heavy it can be to keep going when everything feels pointless. I know what it is like to carry shame, guilt, and silence. And I know how powerful it is to be seen, to be heard, to be met with empathy instead of judgement.

Everyday I keep healing, I get one step closer to that goal. And I carry the pain I have lived through like a lantern, not something I want to relive, but something I can use to light the way for someone else.

From The Inside Out

Part 5- Hope Without Pretending

I will not pretend I have everything figured out, healing has not been a straight line, more like a slow uneven path with days where I still feel stuck, tired, or unsure. But the difference now is, I keep going, I keep choosing to stay, I keep choosing me.

There was a time when I could not see a future at all. Now I am building one, not perfect, not always easy, but mine. A future where I become a peer support worker, not because I want a job but because I want to try and make a difference. I want to be the person I needed when I felt invisible. I want to be the one who says, "You do not have to explain, I understand, I am here."

The darkness still visits sometimes, but it does not own me anymore. I have learned how to sit with it without letting it consume me.

If you are reading this and you are in that place, the empty aching place where everything feels like too much, I want you to know this.

You are not alone, you are not weak, you are not broken. You are human, your story is not over yet.

Hold onto that when the darkness feels endless, remember there is light, even if it is just a flicker right now. Healing is slow, everyone heals in their own time, but it is possible. And there are people who see you, hear you, and walk with you.

I am still healing, still growing, still becoming the person I was always meant to be. And no matter how long it takes, I will get there, when I do I will be ready to walk alongside you. And others, not as someone above them, but as someone who has been in the dark too, and knows how to carry light, to be with you and listen.

Chloie x

The Room Inside Me

There is a room inside of me, locked, windowless, silent. I do not remember the day I built it, only that it has always been there.

I keep it hidden behind smiles, casual conversations, and half laughs that never reach my eyes. It holds the things I never say, the things I do not let anyone see. I tell people I am fine, but inside that room I have screamed into the dark, I have replayed mistakes on an endless loop.

I have memories so tightly they burned into my hands and I keep them all there, regrets, fears, words I wanted to say but swallowed. They rattle the walls when it is quiet. They haunt me, but I do not let them out. Because what if I did? What if someone saw them, really saw me? What would they think of the truth I hide? So I carry this room everywhere. I dress it up with sarcasm, with strength, with being the one that holds it together. No one asks what's inside, no one wants to know.

Sometimes I forget it is there. I move through the day like I am floating, smiling, replying, performing the part. But the moment I am alone, the door starts shaking again. Like something inside me is begging me to breathe. And I do not know if it is trying to escape, or it just wants me to look at it and say, "I see you."

There are memories sealed in there I wish I could forget, things I have said, things I should have said, things I did, moments when I let people down, and times when I let myself down even more. They press against the walls like shadows, familiar, heavy, they do not scream, they whisper, that is worse.

And some of what is in there? It is not dark. It is good things, unspoken love, real dreams I never chased, the versions of me that might have been. They haunt me too; they remind me that silence does not just hide the pain, it hides the possibility.

But I have learned something lately, the door is not as strong as I thought. Every time I speak the truth even just a little it cracks, every time I cry without apology, every time I write what

I am really feeling, every time I do not say, "I am fine," when I am not, I hear the lock loosen, just a little. The room is still there, maybe it always will be. But now for the first time in a long time, I am not afraid to hold the key in my hand.

And lately I have started wondering, what if I opened the door, not just for me, but for someone else? Not all the way, not yet, but just enough, just enough to let them see the walls. The scars etched into them, the pieces I have hidden, the ones I thought made me unlovable. The quiet corners I have sat in, thinking no one would ever understand.

What if someone did not flinch? What if they stepped inside me and just stayed? No fixing, no judging, just, stayed. It terrifies me to be seen like that. But it also softens something in me, because maybe the room is not just a prison, maybe it is also a place of truth.

And maybe letting someone in, is not the same as letting myself fall apart.

Maybe it is how I start to come back together.

The Room Below

A Story about identity, healing and the journey back to self.

Part 1- The fall

They told me healing was a straight road, a clear path you walk from darkness into light.

But my experience was nothing like that, inside my mind, it was more like a spiral staircase, twisting endlessly downward, each step heavier than the last. The air grew colder and thicker. My thoughts repeated themselves, stuck in a loop, like a broken record playing the same sad song over and over.

Some nights I lay awake staring at the ceiling, my chest tightened with a weight I could not name. The world around me blurred into silence. I felt invisible, like a ghost trapped in a body that no longer felt like mine. The masks I wore to protect myself began to crack, and I did not know who was left beneath them.

Then came the breakdown, it was a slow surrender. My body gave into the exhaustion, I stopped pretending, I stopped moving, the person I thought I was collapsed inward.

One evening, after spending hours looking into the dark, I closed my eyes and let the tears fall freely for the first time in years. In that moment of stillness, I found a strange pull, a calling to look deeper inside. That night my mind opened a door I had not dared to approach before. I found myself standing at the top of a stone staircase, spiralling down into shadow and silence. With trembling feet, I descended into a place beneath the noise of the world. The walls glowed, a faintly warm amber light reflecting on the smooth stones. The air smelled faintly of earth and rain, calming and familiar. In the stillness, I heard a small voice, gentle but persistent.

There she was.

A little girl sitting cross legged on the cold stone floor. Her hair tangled and wild, her eyes wide and wet, my eyes. She clutched a threadbare rag doll close to her chest, as if holding onto something precious and fragile. "You finally came," she whispered, her voice both a question and a relief. My heart clenched. "Alice?" I asked, the name a secret I had forgotten I carried. She nodded slowly, "I have been waiting for you."

Part 2- Remembering Alice

I sat down beside her, the little girl named Alice, feeling the weight of years I had tried to forget pressing into my chest. The silence stretched between us, thick with memories unspoken.

"Why are you here?" I asked softly, afraid to break the fragile moment. Alice looked up at me, her eyes steady and unwavering. "Because you left," she said simply. "You tried to forget me when things got too heavy, when the world became too much. But I am the part of you who remembers, who remembers before the masks, before the pain." I swallowed hard. "I am tired, Alice, I am so tired." Her small hand reached for mine, warm and real. "I know, I have been carrying it too," she said.

Her presence felt like a lifeline in a sea of confusion. She was the part of me I had buried deep, my innocence, my truth, my first sense of self before the world told me who I should be.

"You built walls," she said quietly. "To keep yourself safe. But you locked me in here, and you locked yourself out."

I blinked back tears, "I did not mean to forget you, I thought it was the only way." Alice smiled gently. "I know but it is time to remember now, come see."

Together we stood, and she took my hand, guiding me through the glowing corridor that stretched endlessly beneath my mind. The air shimmered with possibilities, and I felt something I had not in a long time, Hope.

Part 3- The Door Of Truth

Alice led me deeper into the glowing corridor, her small hand holding a compass guiding me home. The walls hummed softly, alive with memories, and emotions, my memories and emotions, ours. long buried beneath layers of silence. At the end of the hallway stood a simple wooden door. It was unadorned except for a single word carved into its surface, deep and deliberate, “TRUTH”.

I hesitated, my hand was hovering over the worn handle, “What is behind this door?” I asked, voice barely a whisper. Alice looked at me with steady eyes. “The part of you, you are still afraid to face. The sadness, the shame, the angry part of you, my little brother, the older version of you who grows with you, the questions you never say aloud,” she said.

I swallowed even harder than last time. The question burned inside me, one I had whispered to myself in my darkest moments. Who am I, who am I truly?

She nodded as if she had my unspoken fears. “Let's find out together.”

With a breath heavy as the weight of years, I opened the door. Inside was a room filled with fog and silence. Shadows moved just beyond the edges of my vision. In the centre, a large mirror stood, its surface rippling like water. As I stepped closer the mirror reflected not one face, but many. Different versions of me flickering across the glass, each wearing a different mask, each holding a different story.

There was the confident smile i showed the world, the quiet one who kept secrets, the broken one who disappears when no one was looking, the alcoholic one who drinks to hide them true self, the teenage version of me Chloie still hiding away, the teenage version of me who turned into mr angry, the fighter the one who destroys, then the frightened child who still hoped for love, i could see Alice's face looking into the mirror she knows them all.

The room whispered in many voices only I could hear.

“You are not broken, You are becoming.”

Alice squeezed my hand. “You do not have to be perfect to be whole.”

Tears ran freely now, but they no longer felt like weakness, they were the first steps toward healing.

Part 4- The Mask

In the middle of the room stood a mask. It was beautiful, delicate and shimmering, but broken in places, cracked from years of wear. The mask looked like something I had worn a thousand times, maybe more, the face I showed the world to hide the pieces I did not want anyone to see. I reached out, fingers trembling, and picked it up. It felt heavy in my hands, heavier than I remembered. Holding it, I understood for the first time how much effort it took to keep the mask in place. How exhausting it was to pretend to be someone else. Alice watched quietly. "The mask kept you safe." she said softly. "But it also kept you trapped." I thought of all the times I had behind it, all of the years afraid that if I took it off. No one would recognize me, or worse, no one would want me. "But I do not want to hide anymore" I whispered.

Alice smiled gently, "You do not have to, not anymore." I slowly removed the mask and placed it on a nearby table. For the first time in a long time, I looked at my reflection, not the polished guarded face, but the real me. Vulnerable, scarred, uncertain, but alive.

"I am still here," I said to my reflection. "I am still me." Alice stepped forward and took my hand "And I am still here too, we are all coming home." Together we turned from the mirror and walked through the door, ready to face the next step of the journey.

Part 5- The Message

As Alice and I moved beyond the room with the mask, the corridor shifted again. This time the walls were lined with hand written letters, notes folded carefully, and scraps of paper pinned to a soft corkboard that stretched farther than I could see. Alice reached up and pulled one free. "These are messages, things you have tried to say. But no one listened, things you needed to hear, but no one said."

I unfolded the note carefully, the words were shaky, raw, written in my own hand writing but from a place I hardly recognized.

"I am tired of pretending, I do not know who I am anymore, I do not know if I am alive or dead, I do not know what is real or not anymore, I am scared to be me."

The vulnerability of these words hit me like a wave. I traced each letter, feeling the pain and hope tangled together. Alice's voice was gentle, "You wrote that when you did not know where to turn. But you kept writing, you kept trying." More letters appeared in my mind, letters of love, anger, confusion, and forgiveness. I realized these were pieces of my soul reaching out, trying to connect through the noise. I folded the letter back up and looked at Alice. "Will I ever understand all of this, all the different personalities of me I have tried to hide?" She nodded with certainty, "Understanding comes slowly, one message at a time. And the messages are always there, waiting for you to listen."

In that moment, I felt fragile, a thread of hope weaving itself through the darkness. Maybe, just maybe, the story I was living was not over yet.

Part 6- The Forgotten Garden

The hallway opened, and before me spread a garden unlike any I had ever seen, but I had regularly in my dreams, not good dreams, dreams I was ashamed of but did not understand. Dreams that haunted me for years made me feel guilty. This garden though was not neat and tidy, but wild and free.

Flowers of every colour pushed through cracks in the stone path, vines curled up the wall, heavy with blossoms and leaves. The air smelled sweet and earthy, filled with the soft hum of life returning.

Alice walked beside me, her bare feet brushing the cool grass. "This is your garden," she said quietly, "The part of you, you forgot. The place where all your truths live, even the ones you buried deep." I looked around, surprised at how familiar it felt. This garden was a secret inside me, a hidden refuge where pain and beauty grew side by side.

We walked to a willow tree standing tall in the centre. Its long branches swayed gently, like fingers brushing the air. Beneath the tree was a small mound, covered in soft moss and wildflowers. Alice knelt beside it, "This is where you buried me once." she said softly. "Not because you wanted to, but because you did not know how to hold on to all of us." My throat tightened, the image of burying my inner child, my true self, came back in a flood of memories. I had dreamt this for years but did not understand it. I had tried to live as someone else, trying to fit the world's expectations, hiding the parts of me that did not belong. "But this garden is alive," Alice continued. "It is waiting for you to come back to heal."

I knelt beside her, feeling the earth beneath my hands, the roots beneath the soil were tangled but strong. Life was pulsing there, unseen but unstoppable.

"Can we grow again?" I asked, voice trembling. Alice smiled, eyes bright with hope. "Always, this your garden now, Always this is our garden now."

Part 7- The Place She Was Buried

Beneath the willow tree, the earth was soft and warm beneath my fingers. I could feel the pulse of something alive, a memory buried too deep but never gone. The mound was not just a place it was a story, a secret whispered between the soil and the sky.

"I thought I had to bury you," I whispered to Alice, my voice breaking. "Because I did not fit into this world, because I was afraid." she nodded gently. "You buried part of yourself to survive. To protect what you could not yet understand." The truth hung between us like fragile glass. I remembered the years of trying to live as someone I was not, the years of hiding who I really was because the world demanded it. Being intersex, growing up expected to be a boy, it felt like I was split in two, torn between selves that never quite aligned. "But it was not the end." Alice said softly "It was a pause, a breath before the next chapter."

I closed my eyes and felt the weight of their buried years. And then in that quiet moment, I made a promise "this is not a burial anymore," I said voice steadying. "It is the beginning." Alice smiled, her small hand resting over mine. "And now we are going to grow together now."

Part 8- The Becoming Ritual

In the heart of the garden, Alice and I gathered stones, petals, and fallen leaves. Together we created a circle on the soft earth, a sacred space to honour all the different visions of me, all the versions I had been, all the versions of me that exist inside of me.

The ritual felt ancient and new all at once. We lit a small fire in the centre, the flames flickering like fragile hopes. Alice handed me a piece of worn paper, the letter I had once written, filled with fear and doubt.

With reverence I held it over the flames. The paper curled and burned, smoke rising upward, carrying away the weight of shame and silence. "We let go," Alice said "But we also remember, we do not erase the past, we honour it. Every crack, every scar has shaped who you are."

Then she handed me a small seed, dark and round. "This is your promise, the seed of who you are becoming." I pressed the seed into the earth at the centre of our circle, feeling the soil close around it like a warm embrace.

"I choose you now." I whispered, "I will never bury you again, none of you."

The garden seemed to breathe with me, alive and waiting this was more than a ritual, It was a rebirth. A gentle, powerful declaration that the true me was emerging, piece by piece.

Part 9- The Circle Of Selves

As the fires glow softened, the garden around us began to shimmer with life. From the shadows, other versions of me appeared, some I barely recognized, others I had feared or forgotten. They gathered quietly in a circle around the ritual fire, each carrying their own stories, their own pain and hope. There was the young child, a boy who once hid behind walls of silence, the angry teenager, young adult who fought to be seen. The quiet observer who learned to survive by disappearing. The brave woman, older, wiser standing tall with kindness in her eyes, me now.

Alice stood beside me, hand steady and warm. "They are all part of you. All the ways you have been, all the truths, the trauma. The hurt you have carried, I looked around the circle, feeling a deep sadness and a powerful love wash over me. I wanted to reach out to each version, to tell them it was ok to rest, to heal, to grow. "I am me now." I said softly "and I am ready to hold all of you."

One by one the versions of me stepped closer. We joined hands, forming an unbroken chain of acceptance and understanding.

In that circle, I found home, a sense of belonging. For the first time in years. The garden whispered around us, the leaves rustling like a lullaby. The journey was not over, there was still the angry one to collaborate with. But the path forward was lit by a gentle light, a light born from love and courage.

Part 10- To Be Continued

The garden stretched before me, endless and wild, full of shadows and sunlight. The seed I planted pulsed, softly beneath the soil, alive with possibility, waiting to grow. Alice stood beside me, no longer a child but a reflection of all I have been and all I will become.

The journey was far from over, there would be days of doubt, nights of silence, moments when the masks might feel like the only safe place again. But now, I knew I had the courage to face those times. The door beneath the staircase remained open, a promise that I could return anytime, that healing was not a destination but a continuous unfolding.

I took a deep breath and stepped forward, hand in hand with Alice, ready to keep growing, one step, one breath, one truth at a time.

A message to anyone like me.

If you are reading this, and you feel lost, fragmented, dissociative, or unseen, please know you are not broken, you are not too much, you are not alone. There is nothing wrong with you for carrying your truth quietly. For surviving however you had to. For wearing masks just to feel safe.

I know what it is like to forget who you are just to be who the world expects you to be. I know the ache of burying parts of yourself that should never have been hidden.

But I also know this.
There is still time.
To return.
To remember.
To become.

Healing is not a straight line. It is a spiral, a garden, a story still to be written. One breath, one step, one gentle truth at a time. You can come back to yourself.

I am Chloie, I am a woman, I am intersex, I am kind, I have dissociative identity disorder D.I.D, I am healing, I am here.

AND SO ARE YOU.

You do not need to have it all figured out. You just need to keep going. Even in the dark, the seed of who you are is still alive. And when you are ready it will bloom.

With all my heart take care of yourselves.

Chloie.

Do You See Me

Some days, I wonder if I even exist.

I speak but my voice fades before it ever lands. It is like I am shouting underwater, muffled, distant, easily ignored. People talk over me without flinching, like I never said a word. Their laughter, their stories, their noise fills the room while I shrink into silence. I try, I show up, I make conversation, ask questions, smile when I do not feel like smiling, but it is like I am made of glass, I am there, but see through, fragile, breakable, easy to overlook. And slowly that kind of silence seeps in, wraps around me, and settles deep. It starts to sound like truth, like proof. That I do not matter.

It hurts in ways I do not know how to explain. It is not one big blow, it is a thousand small cuts. Each time they cut me off mid sentence. Each time un read, or not invited, or spoken too only when they need something. And I start asking questions I wish I did not need to ask.

Why am I even here?

Would anyone notice if I stopped trying?

If this is what friendship looks like, why do I feel so alone?

There are quiet moments, usually where I sit with these thoughts and they get too loud. Moments where I think, If I actually vanished, would it actually matter?

Not in a dramatic way, not some cry for attention just a cold, quiet wondering. And when someone does finally notice I am quiet, they say "whats wrong?" like it just started. Like it has not been building up for months, like I have not been drowning in silence while they walked past me day after day.

I want to tell you sometimes, not for pity, but just to be heard, to scream, "I AM HERE, I EXIST, WHY DO YOU NOT SEE ME?"

But I do not. Instead I nod, I smile, I say, "I am just tired." And they believe me, because that is easier for them, than listening to the truth. And the truth is.

This hurts, it is exhausting to feel invisible. To feel like a ghost in your own life. To carry so many words and have nowhere to put them. But I keep carrying them anyway.

Because if no one listens, even if no one sees me, I know I am still here. That might not feel like enough most days. But it is what I have. And for now, that is what I hold on to.

Coming Back To Life

I remember the beeping first, not the pain, not the lights, just the rhythmic annoying beeping of a machine that was keeping track of the life I did not want. I was still here, I did not want to be. That was the first thought, the second was worse. I have failed at this too.

I wanted the world to stop hurting, I wanted out, I did not want to be a burden anymore, I did not want to keep pretending I was fine. But waking up meant facing everything I had tried to leave behind. And now something new, shame, suffocating shame.

No one tells you how hard it is to face the people who love you after something like this. The look in their eyes, the questions they are afraid to ask, the ones you cannot answer. But someone did sit beside me. A nurse I think. She did not try to fix it, did not ask why? She just handed me a glass of water and said, "You do not have to say anything right now, just breathe."

That moment mattered, not because it healed me, nothing did, nothing did, not instantly, but because it told me I was not irredeemable.

I was still a person, not just a mistake. Healing was slow, agonizing, some days I hated myself for surviving, I hated myself for still hating myself. Music helped me, so did writing, I wrote letters I never sent. I started telling the truth about my feelings in group sessions. I began to say out loud the things I was sure would make people walk away, but they did not.

I learned that what I had survived was not failure, it was the first step back. One day I realized the heaviness had lifted, just a little, just enough to breathe, enough to hope. If you are reading this, if you have been where I have been, please know this.

You are not broken, you are not alone, you are still here, and that matters. I am glad I did not die. Not because everything got better overnight, but because now I know, there is life on the other side of that pain. A real one, a beautiful, messy, painful, worth it life. And I am still coming back to life, every day.

I felt like a failure in life and now a failure in death. I was not even sure what I wanted anymore. I just knew I did not want to be me at that moment. I did not want to face what came next, the questions, the eyes, the guilt. People talk about seeing their life flash before their eyes. That did not happen to me, there were no memories, no final message to loved ones in my head this time.

I just wanted it to stop, the constant pressure in my chest, the noise in my head, the feeling that I did not belong anywhere, not even in my own skin. When I woke up in the hospital, it was not dramatic, it was quiet. I opened my eyes and thought, shit I am still here. There was a part of me that hated that, but there was something else too, something small. I would not call it hope, not yet, maybe more like confusion, like why am i still here? And that question stuck with me.

The next few days blurred, doctors, nurses, questions after questions I did not want to answer. And the truth was I did not have the answers. I had not planned it out, I did not write a note. I was not thinking about anything except ending the pain in my own head.

It is not that I did not love anyone, far from it I loved Zoe with all my heart, I still do. It is just that I could not feel anything since she did what she did. And I just could not feel anything any more. It was like everything had been turned off inside me, I felt empty. But not in a peaceful way, in a dead, inside float through the hours kind of way. But slowly, and I mean slowly something started shifting, not a huge epiphany, just little things.

The nurse who sat with me a little longer than she had too, the psychiatrist who did not try to fix me, just listened like I was not broken. The quiet moment I had in the hospital garden, when I felt the breeze and realized I had forgotten what fresh air even felt like.

There were still dark days, there are still dark days. But something changed when I let myself stop pretending I had to be strong, or happy, or fixed. I started telling the truth about my feelings, first to myself, then eventually to other people. That

I wanted to die, that I had felt nothing, that I hated myself for surviving, and also weirdly, I was glad I survived. It was a confusing place to be somewhere between regret and relief.

But I think that is what coming back to life actually looks like. Not some movie moment. Just choosing to stay one more day, and then another.

I do not have it all figured out, I am still healing. But now I know this, I did not survive because I failed. I survived because deep down I was not ready to go. And that is not weakness, that is strength I did not know I had. Rebuilding did not happen all at once, there was no grand plan, no morning I woke up and thought, right I am going to get my life together now. It was slower than that, messier to be honest, at first I did not want to rebuild. I just wanted to disappear quietly and never be asked to explain myself again.

But I kept waking up and somewhere in that repetition, that still here again feeling. I realised maybe I was meant to.

So I started small, getting out of bed, having a shower, eating something, anything. I did not set goals or force myself to feel motivated. I just tried to do the next thing and then the next, one small thing at a time. I had to relearn how to exist, how to feel things again, and how not to run from those feelings.

There was a lot of guilt, still is sometimes, guilt for what I did, guilt for hurting people, guilt for not thinking of them when I made the choice. But guilt does not heal you, honesty does. And forgiveness mostly of myself started to come when I let go of the idea that I should have done it all differently. I went to therapy, at first I did not say much, I sat in silence, arms crossed, heart closed. But over time I started to speak, slowly awkwardly, and every time I told a little bit more of the truth. The weight of it all got a bit lighter.

I lost people who did not understand, but I also found people who did, people like yourself. People who had been through it. People who did not flinch when I said what I had done, that kind of connection saved me in a different way.

Eventually, I started doing things that made me feel real

again. Writing, walking, music, not for anyone else, just for me. And one day, without realising it I laughed at something, and it hit me I had laughed in months. That was proof, proof I was still here, under all the pain. Proof that coming back to life was not a myth it was possible. If I could go back to the version of me who swallowed those tablets, I would not lecture her, I would tell her that everything happens for a reason or that it gets better, not right away. I would just sit with her. And I would say, "I know it hurts, I know you cannot see past this moment. But please just wait."

Because what I have learned since then is this. Pain lies, it tells you, you are worthless, it tells you no one would care, it tells you nothing will ever change. But pain is not the truth, it is just a part of it, and if you can survive it even barely, even broken, there is more waiting on the other side.

You do not have to be grateful for surviving right away, you do not even have to know why you did it. But you are still here, and that means there is still a chance, a chance to heal, to rebuild, to find pieces of yourself you thought were gone forever. I have learned that being honest saves more lives than pretending ever did. That asking for help is not weakness, it is the bravest thing you can do.

And that even on days when the dark thoughts come back, I am not back at the beginning, I just know what to do with them now. I have also learnt that I am not alone, and neither are you.

If you are reading this and you have ever felt what I felt, that silent, sinking, empty nothing, please believe me when I say.

You are not broken.

You are not beyond saving.

And this moment, no matter how unbearable it is, it will pass. I did not think I would ever come back from what I did. But I did, I am still here, and now I am living a life I never thought I would get to see, not perfect, not painless, but real.

And real is enough.

The Monster Room

There is a door in my mind I try not to open.

Sometimes it creaks open when I sleep, sometimes it slams open like a storm when I am awake. Behind it lives a part of me that is not gentle, that does not cry, does not ask for help, does not beg to be understood. He does not ask for anything he just takes.

I never gave him a name, I do not think he needs one. He does not care what I call him, he only cares about the silence before the scream. He is all sharp teeth and claws made of rage. He burns inside me like wildfire, and when I feel him rise, it is like drawing in heat.

I used to think he was a monster, maybe he still is, but he is also me.

Or at least he is part of us, part of this, he comes out when I can not, when it is too much, when my brain decides no more. Then the light goes out, I wake up in places I do not remember walking too, sometimes in strange places, sometimes on the top of the motorway bridge, sometimes I wake up in the hospital with stitches, taken an overdose, with bruises I did not give myself, with blood that is not always mine.

People ask me what happened, the police, the doctors, people I thought were friends. I never have an answer that makes sense, I just say, I was not there. And I mean I was not there.

But he was.

And I hate that he scares me more than anything in the world, yet sometimes I wish I had his strength. Because maybe if I had it, I would not need him to show up at all. I think he was born from things I was not allowed to feel. All the fury I swallowed, all the fists I did not throw, all the screams I buried. Someone had to carry them. Someone had to survive in ways I could not.

But he is not safe, not for me, not for anyone. I try to build stronger doors, lock them tight, stay present, try and control when I switch, stay grounded, in control. But I always feel him there, pacing, waiting, hungry, and sometimes just before the blackout I hear him whisper. "I will take care of it," like it is a kindness, like I asked, but I did not. And still the hardest truth is this.

Maybe he is not the monster. Maybe the real monster is what made him necessary. And maybe if I am brave enough, I will stop running from him and start learning how to co-exist with him. Without letting him take over.

I woke up in the hospital again, fluorescent lights buzzing, IV in my arm, the antiseptic smell already making me feel sick. Before I even open my eyes. The nurse noticed me waking and gave that tight, polite smile like she has seen this a hundred times before. Like she knew me, maybe she did, I was not sure anymore, I had been here enough.

There was a bandage around my wrist, a bruise blooming over my ribs. I did not remember the pain starting, but I felt it now, real, heavy. I did not ask what happened, I already knew what they would say. "You had an episode, you were out of control, you hurt yourself, you scared someone, you are lucky it was not worse."

They never say you were not alone, they just say you. Like I chose this, like I did it. But it was not me, it was him, Mr Angry. (that is what I call him now).

Because I do not know what else to say. I do not know if he is me, or something I built in my own mind. Or something that built itself out of everything I could not deal with. I do not know if he is a protector, a punisher, or a prison guard, he is just Mr Angry.

I know when he has been here, he leaves everything scorched, people stop calling, my phone has messages I can not read, apologises I can not write because I do not know what I am sorry for. Sometimes I stare at my hands after sometimes for hours, trying to feel like they are mine again. Sometimes I just sit in the quiet, no music, no lights, just silence and breathing and the faint echo of whatever he did. I ask myself the same questions.

Why now?
What triggered it?
How long was I gone?

No answers come, just hear the ticking of the clock, and sometimes if I listen really closely, I hear him, not shouting, not roaring. And all I feel is just the ache, the exhaustion. Feel him just breathing. Somewhere deep in the dark of my mind, still there waiting and I wonder, what happens if I stop being afraid of him? What if I try to talk to him? What if he is not a monster at all, just a part of me no one ever taught how to be human.

I do not have answers yet, but I am here, I survived and for now that is enough. After the hospital, I went home, or at least to the place I live. It does not always feel like mine. The walls are mine, the bed is mine, the clothes, the lights,the toothbrush. But I do not always remember buying the groceries. I do not remember folding the laundry. Sometimes I open drawers and find things I did not know I owned.

That is when it starts again, Mr Angry does not come roaring this time, "You should have let me finish, you are weak, they do not care about you, let me out again, let me protect us.

And if I let that voice in, even just a little, others start coming too, fast, jumbled, loud. We can not do this, he is going to get us killed. Shut up all of you, let someone else front, no one listens to me any way, why are we even trying anymore?

It builds like a wave, like thunder rolling behind my eyes. I do not always know who is talking, sometimes they do not have names, just moods, just tones, fear, anger, sadness, blame. Sometimes I try to answer them, but my thoughts get so tangled. I forget even what I was going to say, the words blur, my chest tightens, my fingers shake, my mind splinters. And then I lose time, I have blackouts, hours, days, minutes. When I come back it is like waking up underwater, gasping, drenched in confusion.

That is the part people do not understand, they think D.I.D (dissociative Identity disorder) is like acting, like role playing, like switching costumes in a play. But it is not a performance, it is survival. It is fragmentation, it is chaos in a brain that was not made to carry this much alone. When I have moments of silence, real silence. I cherish them, I sit in the dark, I hold a warm mug in my hands, I breathe, I listen. And if the voices start creeping in, I say out loud, "I hear you, but I am here right now, I am here, I am staying."

It does not always work, but sometimes it does, sometimes I get a few hours of peace. Enough to write this, enough to remember who I am, who we are, without collapsing into the noise.

I still do not know what Mr Angry is, I still do not know what he wants. But I know one thing: he is not the enemy. The chaos is terrifying, but it is ours.

And that means somehow we can survive this.

Betrayal Of The Mind

It is never just one comment, that is the thing people do not get, do not understand.

It is not, "You are quiet today," or, "You look tired," that hurts by itself, it is the pile up. The way one offhand sentence lands in the wrong part of your mind, at the wrong time, and suddenly it explodes. Not outside, inside, quietly, violently. And then you overthink, every word, every silence, every look that felt a little too long.

You start replaying conversations, dissecting tone, questioning why they said it, what they really meant, It is exhausting.

And the worst part is no one sees it, no one gets it, because from the outside? I look fine, I nod, I smile, I keep it moving, but inside? I am spiralling, boiling, and getting angry, not just annoyed, angry short fused, defensive cold. I will lash out, or shut down, or avoid everyone because I do not know how to say. "The things you said broke me a little." Because it sounds stupid right? petty, overreacting.

But it is not just that thing, it is all the things I have bottled up. All the insecurities that have been building, quietly poisoning everything. The way my mind twists words into weapons and hands them back to me. I do not even know who I am angry at most days, them, me, my past, my brain?

Sometimes someone says something and they move on, forget it, go about their day, and I am still stuck there hours later, heart racing, fists clenched. Imagining different ways I should have responded. Thinking about how they probably laughed about it after I left. Even if I know they did not, even if I know it meant nothing.

Knowing does not stop it, if anything it fuels it knowing I have reacted yet again. It is like my brain has got multiple voices, one that wants peace, and one wants to tear everything apart, especially me, the rest just stirring it all up.

I lose trust in people, myself. I distance myself before they get a chance to do it first. I fake being okay as well, I don't even know when I am lying about being okay anymore. I smile at people I am silently resenting, I laugh with them while secretly I am falling apart. I get complimented on being calm, but all I want to do is scream. Because they have no idea how loud it is in here, here in my fragile mind.

And then comes the crash after the storm, the regret, the emptiness, I think, why did I get so worked up, why can I not just be normal? But even with these questions, those questions turn into weapons. There is no mercy in this mind, no room to breathe.

This is what it means to live with a mind that betrays you. It makes you feel broken for feeling too much. It convinces you that no one would understand, that no one cares. Maybe they shouldn't, why should they.

And I do not have a neat ending for this, no break through, no healing arc.

I am just surviving it, not living just existing, day by day. Trying not to hate myself for being affected by things that should not matter.

Trying not to explode on people who do not know what they have stepped on. Trying not to let my mind win, some days I win, some days my mind wins.

But I am still here, still fighting it, still breathing through the betrayal of my mind.

The Strings Between Us

The nights had stretched out long and indistinct, stitched together by the soft glow of my phone screen and the low hum of a room that never quite slept. My body moved, but not really of its own will. Fingers scrolled without purpose, eyes skimmed photos, headlines, faces, words I did not care about, but still consumed anyway. Time lost shape, hours and minutes blurred, and it no longer mattered which was which.

I felt hollow, a kind of emptiness that was not sadness exactly, more like numbness wrapped in exhaustion, pressing on every part of me. Even breathing felt like an effort, slow and deliberate, as though the air itself was heavy.

Somewhere nearby my guitar leaned against the wall, slightly out of tune, gathering dust, like a memory I was not ready to touch. I could feel its presence in the corner of the room, solid and quiet, but I did nothing, I could not.

Sometimes I remembered sound, a melody that had once rolled through my fingers, a chord that had lived in my chest, warm and alive. The memory made my fingers twitch, unconsciously, but the moment passed too quickly, leaving only ache and longing. I did not reach for it. I could not trust the memory to hold me up. Too many years of work, betrayal, and exhaustion had left me frayed and fragile.

I glanced at the phone again. I did not want to scroll. I did not want to stop either, the glow of the screen drew me in, but it did not satisfy, each notification buzzing briefly, a tiny spike in my chest, before fading into nothing. I realised I was just trying to keep the silence at bay. Trying to fill space with meaningless noise because silence felt too heavy, too exposing.

And yet, even in that numbness, something stirred, it was faint, delicate, like the whispers of strings in a dream I could almost reach. A pulse, a memory, a tiny spark reminding me that somewhere beneath this exhaustion, this depression, beneath this endless scrolling, beneath the fog of everything I had endured, something still existed, something worth noticing.

I did not move, I did not play. I simply lay there, aware that the room, the hum, the glow, and the guitar, all of it waited quietly, patiently, as if understanding that my next step would be small. Too small to matter, yet in truth it would matter more than I could yet imagine.

Silence.

Silence was steady, it draped over the room like a thick, dark curtain, soft but unyielding. It told me, without words, that it was safer to stay still, do not risk movement, do not wake, do not let the world in.

I felt its presence in the weight of my body against the sheets, in the warmth of my blanket pressing down, in the slow inhale and exhale that seemed to synchronise with the hum of the heating. Silence did not push, silence only held me.

It observed the small flinches and twitches, my fingers curling, uncurling, hovering near the guitar, and did not interfere, it let me feel the ache without demanding a solution. It let me notice the subtle pulse of memory beneath my ribs, silence reminded me that stillness could be enough, it reminded me that some nights, survival itself was the achievement.

Occasionally, my mind tried to escape, thoughts drifted to unfinished tasks, responsibilities, worries about money, work and everything I had failed to handle, silence folded itself tighter around me and slowed the rush of thoughts. I did not fight it, I let the weight of nothingness settle in my chest.

Even in the quiet, I felt hints of longing, a chord remembered. A melody almost tangible, a vibration that whispered beneath the numbness. Silence noticed it too, but it allowed it to exist, without pushing me toward action. It was a companion that let me simply be, letting the world wait outside the walls of the room.

For hours, I remained in this cocoon, not asleep, not awake, simply present. And in that presence, I felt the trace of something

I had thought lost. The possibility of noticing, of choosing, of moving again, one small step at a time.

Distraction.

Then distraction stirred, it was restless, a spark of movement in the hollowed room. Look, scroll, scroll someone posted something! Someone said something! Something to react to! I obeyed without thought, my thumb flicked across the screen, colours, words faces, outrage, humour, they raced past me.

Distraction fed on the noise on the movement, on the constant tick of small things, happening in the world outside. It did not care if any of it meant anything. It only mattered that I moved, that I did not feel the emptiness too slowly.

Notifications buzzed like tiny alarms, a comment here, a picture there, headlines flashing. Distraction thrived on this rhythm, on the tiny spikes of engagement. And yet, even in the chaos, there was a flicker, a memory of music, of strings, of a note waiting to sound. I felt it briefly, and distraction ignored it.

Impatient.

I realised the push and pull of voices inside my fragile mind. Silence wanted to hold still. Distraction wanted movement, sound connection, anything to keep my body occupied. And somewhere beneath them, music whispered faintly, patient, waiting.

Even while scrolling, I felt the guitar's weight in the room. The memory pressing softly against the edges of attention. Distraction flared, restless and impatient, but I noticed. That noticing, subtle as it was, became the first crack in the wall between numbness and presence.

For the first time in weeks, months, I felt the faintless possibility, I could choose one action, however small, without being pulled entirely by distraction. A moment of quiet awareness in the middle of noise. And that moment, fleeting though it was, felt like a tiny spark of life.

Music.

Music did not need words, it only needed awareness, my fingers twitched nervously. My foot tapped without permission. My chest carried rhythms I had not consciously made. Music remembered, it remembered the weight of the guitar, the warmth of strings, the vibration of sound in my body.

I reached for it carefully almost reverently, the guitar rested cool and solid in my lap. I did not tune it, I did not play a song. I simply brushed one string with my thumb.

The note quivered, shaky, imperfect, but real. Silence stiffened but did not react, distraction paused, uncertain. impatient wanted more, but was patient, music exhaled, a whisper of recognition that stirred in my chest.

I let the hang in the air, longer than it deserved, it was small, it was faint, it was imperfect. But it existed, and in existing, it reminded me of something I had forgotten. That even when my mind was in numbness, and exhaustion, creation was possible, connection was possible, movement was possible. But most importantly it reminded me like the note existed, so did I.

I allowed myself to linger there, hand resting on the guitar, thumb brushing the strings, listening to the sound fade naturally, each note, each vibration, was a reminder, I was not gone, something still lived here in my mind. Something still wanted to move, to create, to survive. My fractured mind was stirring.

Integration/Quiet hope.

I stayed with the guitar longer than I intended, the note hummed faintly beneath my touch, even when I did not play, silence, distraction, in patients, and music sat with me, co-existing, not as enemies or instruction but as part of a whole, I was only just beginning to notice.

Nothing was fixed, nothing was perfect, but a sound had existed. A thread of something human, alive and mine had returned. I did not need to leap, I did not need to solve everything.

I only needed to remain present, even briefly, and let the voices coexist.

I set the guitar down softly, the phone stayed on the table, ignored. I breathed slowly, I was awake, but not yet fully. I was listening, but not yet playing, and yet somewhere beneath the hum, beneath the stillness, beneath the small and trembling notes. I felt a pulse, forward movement, not huge, not immediate, not permanent. But real. A reminder that the music, the life, all of it was still waiting, still possible, still mine.

Author Notes:

If you have read this far, perhaps you see parts of yourself reflected in these pages. You might recognise silence, distraction, and music in your own mind. You might feel numb, exhausted or unsure where to start.

Here are some thoughts to hold gently as you move forward.

1, Start small, motivation grows from actions, not from willpower alone. Even clearing one small corner of a room, picking up a pen or touching an instrument for two minutes is enough to create momentum.

2, Energy comes first. Sleep , movement, and nourishment matter more than ground plan, tiny actions to restore energy make motivation possible.

3, Experiment instead of demanding results. Try something small and see how it feels. One day, one task, one note on a guitar, these experiments build trust in yourself.

4, Celebrate small wins. Even noticing your breath, brushing a string, taking a short walk is progress, give yourself quiet recognition for your achievements no matter how small.

5, Break problems into manageable steps. Money, work, and life can feel overwhelming. Take one tiny action this week, make a list of skills, explore a small earning opportunity, or reach out to one supportive person you trust.

6, Honour your internal voices, some parts of you want stillness, some want movement, some remember joy. None are wrong, listening to them, gently, helps you act safely and wisely.

Change is not instant, life is not perfect. But small consistent steps, rooted in care and awareness, can rebuild connection, confidence, and hope, one note, one action at a time.

Closing Words

The Strength In Fragility.

As this book comes to an end, I want to leave you not in the darkness, but in the quiet warmth that has kept me going. Connections, understanding and the small moments of courage shared between people who get it.

I have learned that fragility does not mean weakness, it means feeling deeply, loving fiercely, and surviving silently. And it takes a special kind of strength to live with a mind that does not always feel safe to inhabit.

Through this journey, I have found others who carry their own storms, people who do not flinch at my truth, who nod when I speak the unspeakable, who have walked beside me not as saviors, but as mirrors and companions. These like minded souls have been the true heroes of this story. Not because they fixed anything but because they stayed.

If you are one of those people, thank you. If you are still searching for them, do not stop. They exist in the margins, in support groups, in whispered late, night texts, in books like this.

We may never be cured, but we can be understood. We can be held, we can

Hold each other.

AND THAT SOMETIMES, IS MORE THAN ENOUGH.

A Note To You, The Reader

Thank you for being here.

Whether you read one story or every word, your presence means more than I can explain. This book was not easy to write, but it felt necessary. And knowing someone like you would be on the other end made the hard parts softer.

If you are walking through your own struggles, I see you. If you love someone who lives with a fragile mind. Thank you for trying to understand. If you found any piece of yourself in these pages, I hope you feel a little less alone now.

Healing is not linear, growth is not loud, and survival quiet, daily survival, is a kind of bravery too often overlooked.

You matter, you are enough. And you are not.

With all my heart.

Chloie x

To You, Who Helped Me Without Knowing

You have shared parts of your story, whether out loud or just by living, and they reached me,

You might think you are not doing enough, or that your struggle means you are broken.

But I want you to know something true:

You have helped me heal.
You made me feel less alone.
You reminded me that pain does not erase beauty and that being soft in this hard world is strength beyond words,

You are loved.
You are needed.
You are already enough.
Exactly as you are.

Thank you, for being here, thank you for being you.

Thank you.

Jill Roberts my true friend
My brothers for being there.
Glyniss who helped me when I was sectioned
The paramedics who came to me time and time again.
The police who talked me out of many situations.
The nurses, doctors at A & E helped me.
My children who understand.
All the staff at Bridewel, just for being you and you are awesome.
All my friends at bridewell you know who you are.
Neil and Lesley at Calmer hearts in Banbury
you have been amazing.
Staff at Orinoco who welcomed me in.
My festival mates. Just for the laughs and the crazy times.

ORIGINAL DRAWING FOR 'FRAGMENTS OF A BROKEN MIND'

I drew this while spending time in a mental home which inspired me to write this book

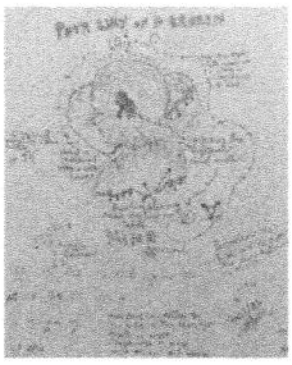

Printed in Dunstable, United Kingdom

78417556R10071